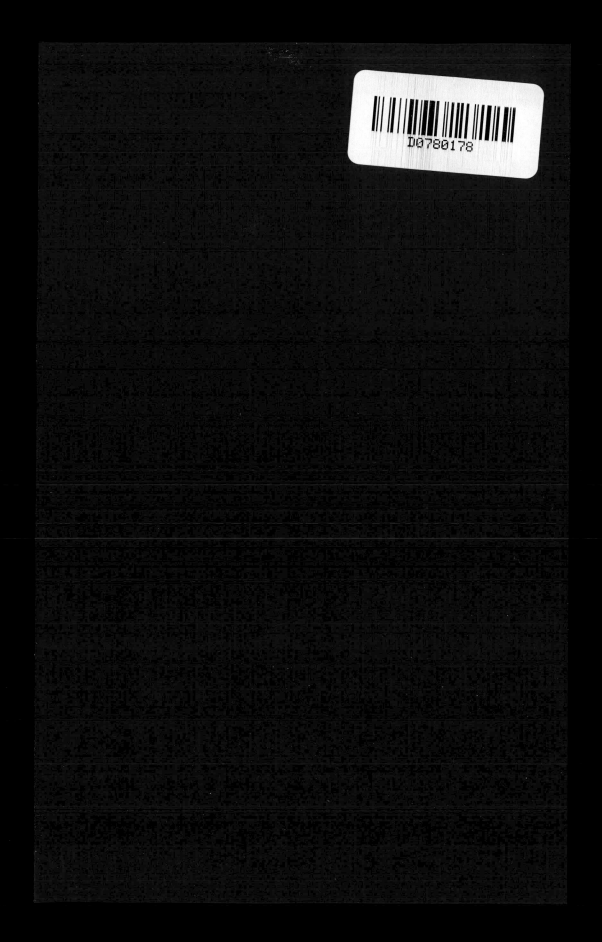

<table>
<tr><td>

...ad cut a wide
...d, that ho had
...n Brown and
...battles of his
...ho Senato, and
...ious speech, in
...vy licks for tho
...ned up conside-
... woll fortifido,
...no through with
...first openin' in
...ruo that Massa-
...y camo in arm
...st havo looked
...r, South Caliny
...y and shiftless
...ors. I think in
...husotts with his
...mouth rock in
...pin and Bunker
...king cano, takin
...r of his country,
...d had to tako
...cultivatin thom-
...o music of Hail
...hor *burning*
...ay bo callod a
...k of hor rained
...nd shou'd havo
...Shado f John
...urn ovor in your
...when you saw
...rostituto horsolf
...ho marridgo had
...or soloctod, and
...tho old story of
...But I s'poso ho
...hod tho spoons
...it was a mar-
...o furnishod hor
...ouch. Alack-a-
...ho couldn't holp
...d had to tako
...tos aro humbled.
...o of Hapsburg,
...Houso of Mis-
...hor health—
...And though, as
...or may prove a
...t with Miss Car-
...iscarriago. Ro-
...*culo matrimonii!*
...r guosts! Draw
...m sloop. Cod-
...nd Charleston!
...Hampton! Pn

</td><td>

tho chickon's crown.

Possum Hollow, Aug. 17, 1866.

LIFE AND DEATH.—Lifo is but doath's vostibulo; and our pilgrimago on earth is but a journoy to tho gravo. Tho pulse that prosorvos our boing boats our dead march, and tho blood which circulatos our life, is floating onward to tho dopths of death. To-day wo soo our friends in health; to-morrow wo hoar of thoir docoaso. Wo clasped tho hand of tho strong man but yosterday, and to-day wo closo his oyos. Wo rodo in a chariot of comfort but an hour ago, and in a fow moro hours tho last black chariot must convoy to us to tho homo of all tho living. Oh, how closoly alliod is death to lifo! Tho lamb that sportoth in tho fiold must soon fool tho knifo. Tho ox that lowoth in tho pasturo is fattoning for tho slaughtor.— Troos do but grow that thoy may be foll- ed. ... os and greator things than thoso fool ... Empiro riso and flourish; thoy flourish but to docay, thoy riso but to fall.

How often do wo tako up tho volumo of history and road of tho riso and fall of ompiros! Wo hoar of tho coronation and of tho death of kings. Doath tho dark sorvant who ridos behind tho chariot of life. Soo lifo, and death risos closo behind it. Death reachoth far throughout this world, and hath stampod all torrostial things with tho broad arrow of tho gravo. Stars dio mayhap; it is said that confla- grations havo boon soon far off in tho othor, and astronomers havo marked tho futuro of othor worlds—tho docay of thoso mighty orbs that wo havo imaginod sot forovor in sockets of silvor to gliston as tho lamps of oternity. But blossed bo God, thoro is ono placo whoro death is not lifo's brothor—whoro lifo roigns alone; "to livo" is not tho first syllablo which is to bo followed by tho noxt "to dio." Thoro is a land whoro tho dark knolls aro novor tollod, whoro gravos aro novor dug. Blost land boyond tho skios. To reach it wo must dio.—*Jackson Mississippian.*

A "TRUE BILL.—Dr. H. Hinkloy, wri- ting from his "Prairie Cottago," Alabama, to tho *Southern Ruralist*, gives, in a fow pithy and portinent words, our agricul- tural noods in tho South:

</td><td>

</td></tr>
</table>

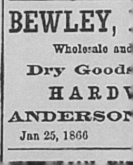

KINGS COUNTY DISTILLERY

DEAD DISTILLERS

A HISTORY OF THE UPSTARTS AND OUTLAWS WHO MADE AMERICAN SPIRITS

x x x

COLIN SPOELMAN AND DAVID HASKELL

ABRAMS IMAGE, NEW YORK

Stacking empty barrels at the J.T.S. Brown distillery (now Wild Turkey)

Distillery Hand
BALTIMORE SUN
MAY 22, 1846

INTRODUCTION

I have become a connoisseur of cemeteries. Bardstown, Kentucky, has two. The good one is near the Old Talbott Tavern. Its jagged stones (the ones that still exist) stick out at odd angles, the grass is not regularly mown, and there are no fences to separate the burying ground from people parking for a quick stop at the bank or to walk the dog. The cemetery can be visited in a minute or two; there's not much left to see but the ancient markers, a small bit of evidence in this little town of life in the eighteenth century. If there are any distillers here, they are likely forgotten.

Most of the known distillers are up the street, at the city cemetery, which is divided into a Protestant and a Catholic section. Jim Beam is buried here, but so are the founders of Maker's Mark and Willett, as well as other, forgotten distilleries, long closed. The city cemetery is more conventional, almost suburban: a wooden gazebo, some long straight avenues that keep an orderly rectilinear plan, very few trees. The only thing unusual about it is the peculiar, persistent smell of bourbon mash, which drifts over from the Barton distillery, half a mile away.

Green-Wood in Brooklyn, dark and overgrown, has a surprising share of distillers. With its grand monuments covered in lichen and soot, showing the wear of proximity to the city, it would take weeks to walk the curving lanes and paths throughout the grounds' 478 acres. Cave Hill in Louisville is cleaner but less grand; its burial markers elegant but less numerous. Spring Grove in Cincinnati has singular large monuments that are spread out like follies in a large gothic garden. The national cemetery in Arlington is a pastoral theme park, with hordes of tourists and school groups wandering in noisy clusters through the ordered grid of government-issue stones. When visiting the grave of Leonard John Rose in Boyle Heights, in Los Angeles, I saw an entire family tailgating at a headstone, a celebratory affair as best I could see from a respectful distance, and a spark of humanity in an otherwise sterile park of grass and stone.

David and I became interested in cemeteries when, in 2011, an employee at Brooklyn's Green-Wood, the first planned cemetery in New York, came up with the idea for a somewhat unconventional tour: a visit to the graves of former distillers, followed by a whiskey tasting at one of the craft distilleries that had recently established themselves in the borough. In the 1840s, New York made as much as 25 percent of the distilled spirits consumed in the country, but that history is largely unknown to current New Yorkers, as distilleries gradually moved south and west, until the political forces around the temperance movement killed the last one some time after 1917. Then, thanks to changes in state laws, a wave of craft distilleries returned to the city. Kings County Distillery, established in 2010, became the first in the city since Prohibition. As distillers particularly interested in this forgotten history, we jumped at the chance.

This tour of dead distillers proved to be strangely intriguing, more than a stunt to attract morbid neighbors or an excuse to drink in the afternoon. There was something humbling to be surrounded by so many distillers in a city that had abandoned the vocation completely for a hundred years. The immersion in death and quietude had a disjunctive effect—reassuring as much as frightening; somehow the cemetery conveyed both a sense of optimism and pessimism. The cemetery felt like a place of great mystery and possibility, a kind of catalog of stories, lost to time.

Exhuming some of the stories of those we visited on the Green-Wood tour—and viewing them in the context of graves and eternity—led to some revelations about our own chosen profession. There is something allegorical about distillers, liquor, and death. Here, we tried to extract from the stories of individual distillers a distinctly American story (and

Green-Wood Cemetery

morality tale), though it is a story without an ending and with a pre-ponderance of subplots. Like the cemetery itself, it is a collection of characters, oddly juxtaposed, arranged more or less chronologically by death date.

x x x

This is a book, then, about distillers who have died. Some are well known, either because their names can readily be found on bottles on liquor store shelves or because the alcohol they made was a footnote to an otherwise memorable life. Others remain nameless, known only to history by an account of their accidental death, written in small-town newspapers at a time when every city was a town and when distillery accidents were common tragedies, as much the stuff of morning papers as the price of vanilla beans, hemp rope, or saltpeter. This book takes a broad view of who can be considered a distiller—a factory hand, a business owner, a salesman, a slave.

Americans have been distilling for almost four hundred years, starting with Dutch businessmen Cornelis Melyn and Willem Kieft, who built the first commercial distillery on Staten Island as an adjunct to a plantation. Jim Beam and Jack Daniel were distillers, of course, but so were presidents George Washington and Andrew Jackson. Industrialists Andrew Mellon and Henry Clay Frick were distillers, but so was Birdie Brown, who lived under the Judith Mountains in Montana and, in 1933, blew herself up while making moonshine as she was dry cleaning. Because alcohol has such a contentious place in North American his-tory, our distillers are heroes or villains, existing uneasily in that space between honest businesspeople and merchants of depravity.

Though disparate in historical and geographical circumstance, these distillers often share common traits: humble beginnings, fierce industriousness, ostracism from prevailing society, personal reinvention, a propensity for exaggeration, a contrarian spirit, indomitable energy, superstition, social insecurity, a surprisingly common affinity for fast horses.

The act of distilling remains more or less the same today as it did in the 1600's, when it first appeared on the North American continent. The technology has not advanced substantively, and while the product has experienced eras of boom and bust, we continue to drink hard liquor in roughly the same quantity as our parents and great-great-grandparents. Because spirits are so often aged, the distiller's art remains a long game, won only after years of toil, and, indeed, sometimes it takes many generations for children to reap the rewards set in motion by their forefathers.

And because the product of distillation—that is, hard alcohol—has often been looked at derisively by the American moral elite, the distiller has often worked in the shadows or at the margins of society. Though federal prohibition against alcohol enacted in 1920 collapsed after only thirteen years, the temperance movement has been a narrative through-line in this country's history, even to the present day. It has been our conscience, scolding us for trying to buy our joy through drunkenness, holding out for the clearheaded America that we have always believed we want to be, a society of ideas.

Spirits, of course, cater not to ideas but to urges. American distillers have very often been immigrants, slaves, Catholics, Jews, hillbillies, women, the poor, or people otherwise marginalized but aspiring to belong. In this sense, the distillers were like their Pilgrim forebears, seeking asylum of a different sort and using their ostracism to their advantage. They offered everyone in society a way to commute the pains of everyday life, and for most Americans, regardless of their status, in the long history of our country, that has been a comfort.

The men and women in this book labored against all odds to make a living and provide for their families. They went to work every morning, first over a copper pot and a cordwood fire in a field, then in a wooden shanty surrounded by iron pipes and steaming vats of swill, and then in brick factories fitted with brass and stainless steel. They were dogged, crafty, and a bit subversive. They argued over prices with a farmer; they feared the tax man; they struggled to get equipment to do what it was supposed to do; and they repeated, year after year, a process by which they took the stuff of our days—the fruits of soil and sunshine,

Laurel Hill Cemetery Gate

Cave Hill Cemetery Gate

and the work of tending and harvest—and converted it into the stuff of our nights—the dinners, dancing, and revelry where we all live and celebrate and commune.

For that gracious act, we do one thing in return: We remember.

x x x

Making whiskey, gin, or rum conjures the unseen substance of a fermented beverage and transforms it to an essence of its antecedent (alcohol) but also something more—something mythological, potent, and dangerous. The process is incontrovertibly capitalist and classically American. It takes items of nominal value, like grain, wood, and water, and renders them into objects of luxury, aspiration, and fantasy. Distillation was one of the alchemists' lasting contributions to society: converting alcohol into an invisible vapor, and then returning the vapor to liquid in a potent (and highly flammable) form. Every distiller is flirting with death—death by scalding, death by explosion. To distill is, literally, to summon the spirit, through an act suffused with risk.

After the work of the distiller is done, the work of the drinker begins. Even the experience of drunkenness itself is a flirtation with death. Alcohol, as a sedative, slows the mind artificially, depressing the nervous system and lulling the body into a kind of a waking sleep, a sensation known as drunkenness. Taken further, the mind will stop recording memories, or will shut down completely, as intoxication becomes acute alcohol poisoning. Over time, the effects of repeatedly indulging in this flirtation with death may become permanent, as the deteriorative effects of alcohol affect cognition, memory, and motor skills. Its flirtation with death is aggregate, and depictions of alcoholics from nineteenth-century temperance tracts make perpetual drunks look like zombies, walking dead through the world.

America was most captivated with inebriation in the middle of the nineteenth century, when distilled spirits consumption per capita was at its highest. Like hypnotism and séances, also popular pastimes of the era, drunkenness offered an activity that, before moving images, recorded sound, and modern information exchange, could offer a reliable diversion into an altered consciousness. Almost two centuries later, it remains enormously appealing.

Throughout the nineteenth century, popular culture embraced this shift toward the macabre and the melancholy. Early Victorian Americans were obsessed with romanticism and mysticism: Séances and hypnotism promised to span the divide between waking life and death, and were explored with regularity. Even President Abraham Lincoln allowed a medium into the White House in an effort to communicate with his son Willie, who died at age eleven about a year into Lincoln's presidency.

Historian Garry Wills describes this period of cultural interest in terms of liminal experiences: twilight, daydreams, premonitions, reveries, omens, and necromancy. This focus manifested itself in all forms of cultural production. "The encouragement of dreamy half-states as revelatory led to the romantics' drastic upgrading of melancholy," he writes. "Once considered a physical disorder and a theologically dangerous attitude, it now became a mark of genius." The country was obsessed with Hamlet; our "luminist" painters learned to explore depth in shadow. And since melancholy was believed to be pedagogical, children were encouraged to visit cemeteries, that "supreme locus of liminality."

The gates of the cemetery, in those days portals between the city and the country as well as between life and death, now serve as thresholds through time—they send us back into a world where distillers are proximate, almost alive again, manufacturing melancholy, liquid liminality.

x x x

The Monumental Bronze Company in Bridgeport, Connecticut, cast tombstones and other funerary statues in zinc from 1874 to 1914. Marketed as "white bronze," the headstones were popular and can still be found in cemeteries all across the United States. Over time, the zinc would take on a bluish hue, adding a touch of color to otherwise white and gray cemetery landscapes. (They are now referred to by cemetery

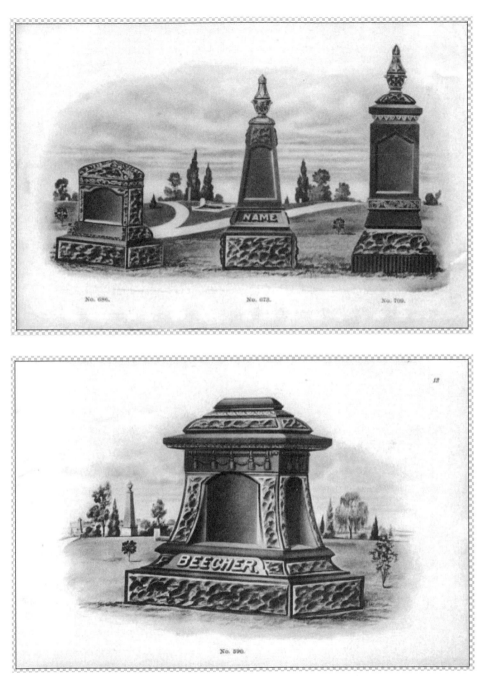

Zinc Tombstone Catalogue

aficionados as "zinkies.") The company was very successful, eventually opening branches in Detroit, Chicago, and Des Moines. The metal headstones were appealing because they were economical, but they were also useful for a reason not obvious at the time: They were hollow.

The story goes like this: A moonshiner, during Prohibition, would bring a few bottles to the cemetery. The headstones of the zinc tombs, though stately, were easy to disassemble. (They had been sold as blanks, with removable panels, so that personalized information could be purchased and installed separately.) Removing these panels revealed a convenient hiding place, one that to the uninitiated was easily lost among a sea of tombstones. It was the perfect drop box. The customer would visit after the fact, find the headstone of the mark, put the cash in the hollow, and take the booze. Whether consumption commenced on the spot was up to the temperament of the customer.

There are published versions of the story associated with cemeteries in Bodie, California; Templeton, Iowa; and Morgantown, West Virginia. It's easy to see how the cemetery might be a good hiding place, though the similarity and lack of detail in all of these stories suggest the trappings of an urban myth. In Green-Wood Cemetery, where there were already more than one hundred thousand interments during the Prohibition years, it is believed by some that the receiving tomb, a grand catacomb not far from the chapel, was used to store illicit liquor (though no one at the cemetery will give the rumor much credence).

But there is at least some hard evidence that cemeteries were trading grounds, if only thanks to their privacy. Paul Ward ran a speakeasy in Washington, D.C. In the documentary *Prohibition,* his son says of a customer, "He brought the hearse up into the back alley, and they put everything in the hearse. And where did they go? The safest place that could be, the Arlington Cemetery. And he had a guard stand by and he paid him money to watch it. Who's gonna stop him? There's a hearse going into Arlington Cemetery. They gonna stop a soldier from being buried? No way."

The idea of the cemetery as a liquor-trading ground represents a serious decline from the heyday, in the middle part of the 1800s, when

American cemeteries were surprisingly fashionable places to see and be seen. Today, we think of cemeteries as lonely places, but perhaps it is useful to think of them as they were in the 1850s, filled with crowds of people promenading and collectively pondering the mysteries of life—a sort of public indulgence in melancholy.

Early settlers were often buried in plain graves near churches. By the early part of the nineteenth century, graveyards became so filled with bodies that soon the number of dead began to outpace the available space to put them. Basil Hall, a sort of travelogue journalist of his day, described conventional burial at the "soppy church-yard, where the mourners sink ankle deep in a rank and offensive mould, mixed with broken bones and fragments of coffins."

The solution arrived in a movement to create rural cemeteries following a pattern set by the ancient Greeks. Mount Auburn, in Cambridge, Massachusetts, was conceived in 1831 as a place of solemnity and quietude outside the city in a specially designed landscape, created for city dwellers to commune not just with lives past but with nature and the eternal future. Cemeteries were designed by horticulturalists, not as gardens but as landscapes, with varied topography, ponds, and gently curved paths.

Mount Auburn was quickly followed by rural cemeteries in Philadelphia (Laurel Hill), Green-Wood (Brooklyn), Green Mount (Baltimore), Spring Grove (Cincinnati), and Cave Hill (Louisville). Often built on high ground with views of the city, these places served as public parks well into the last century. By the middle of the 1800s, Green-Wood Cemetery was one of the country's most visited tourist destination in the United States, with a half million visitors each year, second only to Niagara Falls. Families would come to picnic on the lawns, and visit the statues and architectural follies as public sculpture. Henry Arthur Bright, a visiting Englishman, wrote in 1852, "Cemeteries here are all the rage, people lounge in them, and use them (as their tastes are inclined) for walking, making love, weeping, sentimentalizing, and every thing in short."

In other words, living life. Cemeteries became places where people, by communing with the dead, were able to live their own lives more fully, wandering in the de facto first public parks of the newly built cities. It's not hard to imagine that drinking might have been one of the activities that Bright was alluding to. Cemeteries served as an alternative to taverns or public houses, a place of leisure where anyone could commune with spirits and distance themselves from the city and its demands.

Paddy "Battle-Axe" Gleason, an Irish immigrant and former distiller in Flushing, New York, decided to get out of the distilling business in the late 1860s when the revenue service, in his own words, "tried to compel me to pay $100,000 per month revenue tax." What business did he turn to? "I became interested in the railroad business by seeing on Sundays great crowds of people going to the cemeteries," he said. Gleason made a fortune in streetcars, and became the Boss Tweed–styled mayor of Long Island City.

Of course, the cities often grew to engulf these once-rural places. Walk outside the gates of any rural cemetery today and one is squarely in the city, not the country. But even now, Green-Wood Cemetery remains a pastoral refuge, despite being located a few miles from the Brooklyn Bridge. Spring Grove in Cincinnati might as well be the English countryside, with its rolling hills and wooded valleys that could lose a visitor. At Cave Hill Cemetery in Louisville, the road must be marked with coded lines on the pavement that conveniently allows the visitor to find the way to Colonel Sanders or the exit, but the middle is a warren of knobs, dales, and waterways that make it easy to get lost in the woods with the dead.

Today, stewards of the rural cemeteries, faced with declining revenues as available spaces for burial are filled, are repurposing their grounds, catacombs, and chapels as spaces for parties and cocktail gatherings. Cave Hill Cemetery, with the highest concentration of dead distillers, hosts a bourbon-fueled, cocktails-by-the-lake fundraiser. Green-Wood in Brooklyn has opened its doors for late-night tours, cocktails, and live music in its catacombs. Both cemeteries offer whiskey-history tours.

It is my hope that the reader will visit the cemeteries in this book—the graveyards haunted by the ghosts of distillers long dead—

perhaps thereby rediscovering the Victorian concept of reverie, or a kind of productive daydreaming in the presence of great things. There are maps of a few cemeteries included here for that very purpose. Whiskey or gin may have bought the stone that marks the grave, but one is often prompted to a sense of awe, of reverie, even, not by the stones above the ground, but by imagining the great multitude of loves and lives beneath.

—C. S.

Visitors stroll the Green-Wood grounds
on Decoration Day in 1899

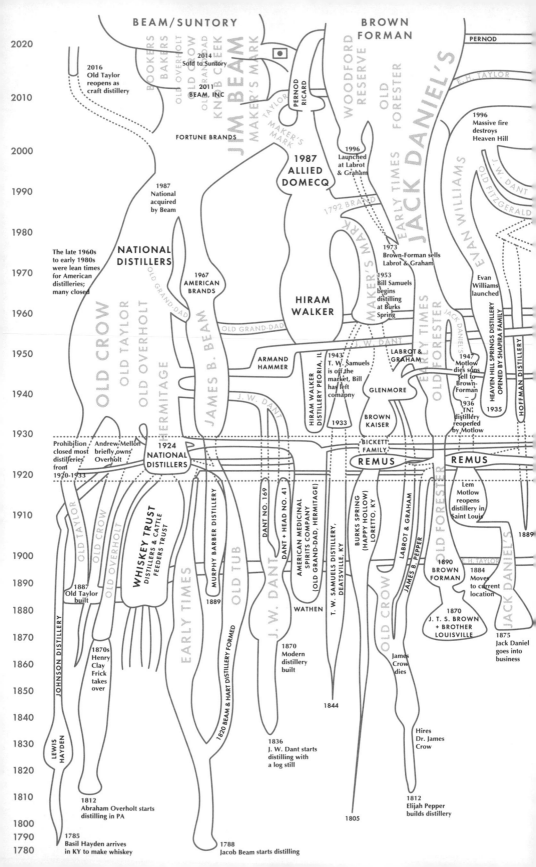

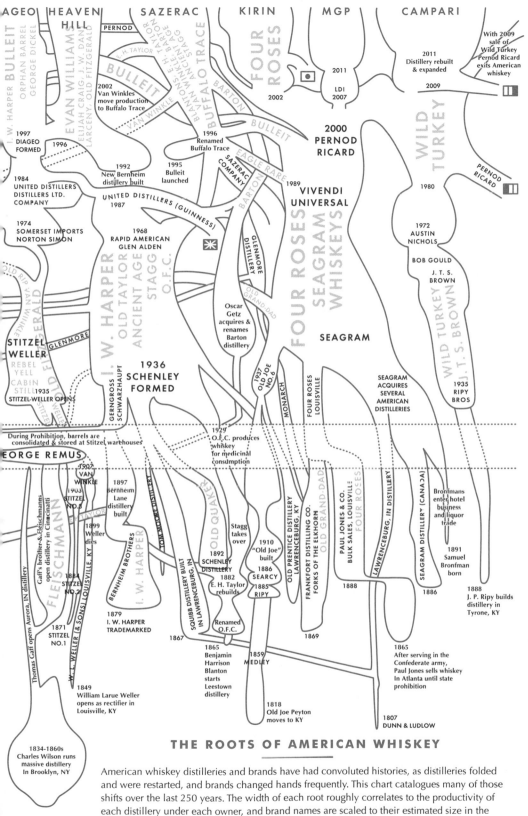

THE ROOTS OF AMERICAN WHISKEY

American whiskey distilleries and brands have had convoluted histories, as distilleries folded and were restarted, and brands changed hands frequently. This chart catalogues many of those shifts over the last 250 years. The width of each root roughly correlates to the productivity of each distillery under each owner, and brand names are scaled to their estimated size in the market based on news reports, historical accounts, and published company narratives.

CAPTAIN GEORGE THORPE

LAWYER, MINISTER, COLONIST

CA. 1576–1622

Berkeley Plantation, Charles City, Virginia

George Thorpe sailed across the Atlantic Ocean on a supply ship to the Jamestown Colony in 1620. In England, he had been—by alternate accounts—a lawyer, physician, minister, and a gentleman, though his journey to America was an opportunity to make even more of himself in the colonies; to be a founder, and, as deputy governor, a leader. Somewhere in the belly of that ship was a small copper alembic still, suitable for making limited amounts of brandy or whiskey. While early settlers were often adventurers, they were also businessmen, and distilled spirits were gaining in popularity. They traveled well (brandy, it has been argued, was invented as a way to transport wine more efficiently), and concentrated the value of fermented products to many times their weight and volume.

Thorpe established residency at the Berkeley Hundred plantation, up the James River from Jamestown. He was charitable and industrious, hoping to learn from the native population as much as he expected to educate them in Christian teachings. He planted vineyards, though he did not live long enough to see them bear usable fruit. In the meantime, Thorpe tinkered with alternative fermentables. At one point, Thorpe wrote a cousin, "Wee have found a waie to make soe good drink of Indian corne I have divers times refused to drinke good strong English beare and chose to drinke that."

Some early accounts of whiskey in the United States describe the spirit as "corn brandy." In context, Thorpe seems to be writing about corn beer—still popular as *chicha* in South and Central American countries—and not its distilled brother, which today is corn whiskey or aged bourbon. Still, the idea of distilling fruit, grain, and molasses were very much on the minds of colonists. Whether Thorpe ran his beverage through his still is not known, but it's plausible, if maybe unlikely, that Thorpe was America's first distiller. (The first record of a commercial still in the New World was twenty years later and 350 miles north, in New York City.)

Thorpe spoke well of the native population. In one incident, the Indians complained about English dogs, and Thorpe ordered them killed in front of their owners as a gesture of respect. He felt no need to flee when the Powhatan Confederacy began attacking settlements in a concerted effort in March of 1622. Thorpe was approached under a friendly pretext by unarmed assailants, and then killed with whatever farm implements were at hand, his body mutilated to send a bloody message to survivors. The Powhatan were known to scrape the brains from settlers' skulls with mussel shells, stuff their mouths with bread (as other settlers were starving), or flay the skin from their bodies before burning them alive. Corpses were tied to a tree or dragged around the property. A mostly peaceful people, the Powhatan employed infrequent violence to maximum effect.

When Thorpe's possessions were inventoried, the copper still was estimated to be worth three pounds of tobacco.

Powhatan attack in 1622

WILLEM
KIEFT

DUTCH MERCHANT, TANNER,
DIRECTOR GENERAL OF THE
DUTCH WEST INDIA COMPANY

1597–1647

———

Interment unknown

CORNELIUS
MELYN

FARMER,
DISTILLER

1600– CA. 1663

———

New Haven, Connecticut, possibly

W illem Kieft came to Manhattan in 1638 as director general of the
Dutch West India Company, following his predecessors Wouter
van Twiller and Peter Minuit, who had famously purchased the island
for a sum of sixty guilders—or twenty-four dollars, in 1855—when the
math was first calculated (today that would be maybe $650).

Kieft arrived at a time when the Dutch settlement was struggling
financially and had just instituted a policy of free trade—a boon to citizens
but a conundrum for his position, which required him to show profits to his
superiors, who expected the company to produce revenue from tariffs and
taxes. The town of New Amsterdam had about four hundred inhabitants
in 1640 and was bounded neatly by the Hudson River, the East River, and
a line of fortifications that gave Wall Street its first meaning. To the north,
the island of Manhattan was mostly uninhabited farmland and woods,
crosscut by Indian trails. The Dutch viewed their colonial settlements more
as trading posts than social utopias, and as such, it attracted the outcasts
from the New World's other beachheads who filled the young port with
many languages and cultures. Liberal and industrious from the start, New
Amsterdam aspired to a culture of an open mind.

Kieft himself was touchy and belligerent. The son of a wealthy
and connected family (a cousin is depicted in Rembrandt's *The Night
Watch*), he hoped to reverse earlier business failures in the new colony
and build sustainable business, mostly in the form of plantations. David
de Vries, a successful farm manager, offered to try to set up a permanent
settlement on Staten Island, which he orchestrated in 1639. De Vries
never lived on the island, but the following year he received reports

from his farmers that the Raritan Indians had made off with one of his pigs, a claim that he relayed to Kieft at dinner. This sparked concern. Kieft sent a raiding company of upward of one hundred soldiers to the Raritan village, killing some men who denied any involvement with the stolen hog. Not long after this incident, the Indians retaliated and burned de Vries's settlement to the ground, killing four settlers, not without clarifying that it was Kieft's own soldiers who had taken the hog while stopping to cut wood and find water on a trip to Philadelphia.

In rebuilding the settlement, Kieft installed a distillery and buckskin tannery near the same site. Cornelius Melyn arrived the next year, 1641. A hopeful businessman with experience in leatherwork, Melyn had been granted the right to develop Staten Island and take over the programs Kieft and de Vries had established. This included managing the distillery.

Pavonia Massacre

What was being distilled is a matter of speculation. We know the settlers grew peaches, which prompted another, more protracted skirmish with the Indians in 1655. So peach brandy is a possible product. Melyn wrote about the grapes he found in his 1650 tract *Representation from New Netherland and Broad Advice*:

> The grapes comprise many varieties, some white, some blue, some very fleshy, and only fit to make raisins of, others, on the contrary, juicy; some are very large and others small. The juice is pleasant and as white in some as French or Rhenish wine, in others, it is a very deep red, like Tent, and in some paler. The vines run much on the trees, and are shaded by third leaves, so that the grapes ripen late and are a little sour, but when the people shall have more experience, as fine wines will undoubtedly be made here as in any other country.

Fruit, however, was more difficult to come by than grain, and most likely what was going into the still was beer. (Grain matures in a single season, and fruit trees and vineyards can take years to reach maturity.) Beer was so prevalent in the colony that Kieft created a law restricting beer purchases during church services or after nine in the evening, and there are reports of Kieft's predecessor encouraging the consumption of beer by example.

Assuming it was beer that Melyn fermented, his distillate would be what we would today call white whiskey. We do know that in 1644, after an exchange of liquor, the Lenape tribe attacked the settlement and burned the distillery and other buildings. Melyn was forced to flee to Manhattan, and the distillery project was abandoned.

Kieft began making enemies of the settlers as much as the Indians. (Limiting when and where people could drink didn't sit well, and his belligerence with the Indians worried many.) By 1647 he was recalled and replaced, and the leading figures of the community, including Melyn, were embroiled in a bitter dispute with the appointed leadership. By the time Peter Stuyvesant was appointed to replace Kieft, Melyn had been charged with treason and sentenced to death. In a strange twist of fate, Kieft and Melyn sailed back to the Netherlands on the same boat, hoping to clear their names, each in his own way. The ship sailed into the Bristol Channel, off the coast of Wales, and ran aground in a heavy storm that battered it to pieces. Kieft drowned; his papers were lost. Melyn miraculously made it ashore as one of the twenty-one souls who survived (107 were aboard).

Melyn petitioned for clemency and returned to New Netherland, but his dispute with Stuyvesant persisted. He eventually settled in New Haven, where it is assumed he died around 1663.

x x x

SON OF JOSEPH WINSHIP, JR.

ACCIDENT—*Last week, a son of Mr. Joseph Winship, Jr. about 14 years of age, accidentally fell into one of the cisterns of Mr. Butlers distillery, and was scalded in such a manner that he expired in a few hours.*

PHILIP LIVINGSTON

DISTILLER,

SIGNER OF THE DECLARATION OF INDEPENDENCE

1716–1778

Prospect Hill Cemetery, York, Pennsylvania

B orn in Albany, Philip Livingston ran a distillery in what is today Brooklyn Heights. Livingston was a Yale graduate and a Manhattan-based lawyer, merchant, and slave trader whose family controlled nearly 250 square miles of land before the Revolutionary War. He built a country house in Brooklyn around 1765 on a hill overlooking New York Harbor. His distillery was sited at the foot of the hill, on the waterfront, and it is speculated to have made gin or genever (a Dutch-style predecessor to gin that is slightly more flavorful). Ships from the West Indies docked here, and sugar was also refined on-site, suggesting instead that the distillery might have made rum, which would have been more consistent with the products of other distilleries of the era.

By 1755, a map of Manhattan depicts seven distilleries operating, but it seems that Livingston took advantage of Brooklyn's remove to create a larger operation, and this made him very wealthy. It also made him a target during the Revolutionary War.

After the fall of Brooklyn and New York in 1776, the British Army took command of Livingston's property. They used the distillery facilities to make beer flavored with juniper berries (a sort of gin-beer hybrid), and converted Livingston's large mansion into a wartime hospital. Those who did not survive were buried on the property, and Brooklyn Heights residents found bones in their gardens through the early 1800s.

Philip signed the Declaration of Independence in 1776 but died shortly thereafter at a convening of the Continental Congress in York, Pennsylvania, as a result of "dropsy of the chest." He was survived by his cousin Robert, who negotiated the Louisiana Purchase for Thomas Jefferson, and his brother, William, who would sign the U.S. Constitution and serve as governor of New Jersey.

This woodcut was included as part of an early temperance tract by George Barrell Cheever

JAMES KINNEY

AND

PATRICK MURTAUGH

MEPHITIC VAPORS.—*It appears from the Coroner's inquest, that two laborers, of the names of James Kinney and Patrick Murtaugh, yesterday lost their lives by imprudently descending into a cistern of the Eagle Distillery, in Perry St. What a capital fact would this have afforded the learned corporation committee on internments, to show the danger of allowing the use of vaults in this city, had it only happened before they published their report? It would, at least, have been as much to the purpose, as the principal facts contained in that daring imposition upon the public; as shall hereafter be shown at full length.*

GEORGE WASHINGTON

GENERAL, PRESIDENT, DISTILLER

1732–1799

Mount Vernon Estate, Mount Vernon, Virginia

The fact that George Washington distilled whiskey is not his most significant contribution to American history, though many have used it to bolster both sides of the temperance debate over the centuries. The story begins, perhaps, with young George prowling around Western Pennsylvania in 1754, ostensibly to provoke the French at the fort at Pittsburgh and assert a claim to the territory for the British. Washington crossed a small river at a site that would eventually become one of the largest distilleries in the country, at Broad Ford (see Henry Clay Frick, page 96). After a little skirmish near Fort Duquesne, the French stronghold in Pittsburgh, Washington retreated to what was later called Fort Necessity, essentially a circle of wood pickets in a meadow situated in a mountain pass, and the most defensible position from which to await supplies. Those supplies never came, and Washington's troops ran out of everything except whiskey. When the French arrived, they were eager for action, but Washington found himself outmatched (and his troops, having broken into the liquor stash, were not in the best condition to fight); he surrendered for the only time in his career. One would think Washington might have blamed the whiskey on his loss, but quite the opposite: Washington became increasingly convinced that whiskey was an imperative resource for a successful army.

After the Revolutionary War broke out in 1775, with Boston and New York in British control, Washington found himself entrenched in a long struggle. Two years in, he wrote to William Buchanan, who was in charge of army supplies:

> It is necessary, there should always be a Sufficient Quantity of Spirits with the Army, to furnish moderate supplies to the Troops. In many instances, such as when they are marching in hot or Cold weather, in Camp in Wet, on fatigue or in Working Parties, it is so essential, that it is not to be dispensed with. I should be happy if the exorbitant price, to which it has risen, could be reduced.

Washington also proposed the erection of public distilleries to keep the price of liquor steady, so that armies might not be reliant on imports. This idea never gained traction, though what a different country we might be living in if it had.

After the war, Washington and his fellow founders were left to figure out how to structure the country, pay for the services it would provide, and deal with Revolutionary War debts, which by 1790 were close to a million dollars. Washington's Secretary of the Treasury Alexander Hamilton had proposed an excise tax that infuriated distillers on the frontier. When Pennsylvania farmers turned a protest on the distiller's tax into an open rebellion (see John Neville and James McFarlane, page 39), Washington found himself back in the neighborhood of Fort Necessity, though he only marched as far as Cumberland, Maryland, before handing over the army to Light-Horse Harry Lee (father of Confederate general Robert E.) and Alexander Hamilton.

After the rebellion subsided and with his presidency over in 1797, Washington returned to Mount Vernon and built there what was probably the largest distillery in Virginia. It's also the most well-documented of any distillery from the eighteenth century in America, and thus provides great insight into distilling technology at the time.

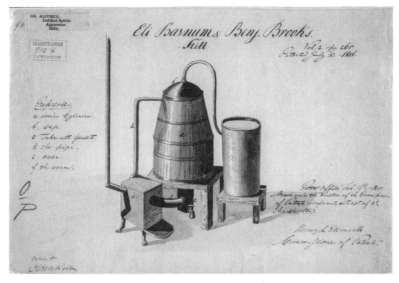

A patent for a still filed with the U.S. Trademark Office in 1808

Washington's farm manager, James Anderson, was a Scottish immigrant who had experience distilling in his home country. In 1797, Anderson urged Washington to let him set up two small stills in the plantation's cooperage, and the six hundred gallons of whiskey he made that year convinced Washington to commit more seriously to the endeavor.

The new 2,250-square-foot distillery was laid out adjacent to the gristmill and eventually would have five copper stills making as much as eleven thousand gallons of whiskey a year (about the size, measured by output, of Kings County Distillery today, or about a third the size of Jack Daniel's first distillery). Washington was concerned about the location near the mill, which was some two miles from the Mount Vernon residence, since there were "idlers" who might rob the still, but given the water source, there was no better location. Washington also sought the advice of John Fitzgerald, a rum distiller in Alexandria, as to the potential profit of the enterprise. Fitzgerald advised him that as long as Anderson was up to the task, he should proceed.

Washington's whiskey was made with 60 percent rye, 35 percent corn, and 5 percent barley that was malted on-site. This makes Washington's rye whiskey not unlike most made in the United States today, though his was often sold unaged, or lightly aged. The common whiskey was twice distilled and cost about fifty cents a gallon, but more expensive versions were three- and four-times distilled and could cost twice as much. Anderson's son John lived near the distillery and did some of the distilling, though much of the work was carried out by slaves Hanson, Peter, Nat, Daniel, James, and Timothy. Washington's distillery also made a small amount of brandy from peaches, apples, and persimmons. Some whiskey was infused with cinnamon. Like many distilleries of the day, the spent grain was useful as feed for Washington's farm animals, especially pigs. The distillery supported 30 cows and 150 pigs that could, according to Polish visitor Julian Ursyn Niemcewicz, "hardly drag their big bellies on the ground."

Washington himself didn't drink much in the way of distilled spirits, preferring Madeira and a certain Philadelphia porter made by Robert Hare, which he often requested by special order. Washington had his own beer recipe, so one could imagine him taking a curious interest in the distilling business. But Washington was already an old man when his distillery came along, and though he was generally pleased with its success, he expressed a clear ambivalence in his correspondence on the topic. One guest from this era noted that Washington rarely spoke, though wine seemed to make him more jovial. That may also have been because Washington's dentures, which were made not of wood but of the teeth of slaves, were so painful that it was easier to be seen and not heard. That is, until alcohol lessened the discomfort.

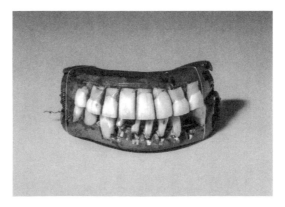

Washington's teeth

JOHN
NEVILLE

DISTILLER,
TAX COLLECTOR

1731–1803

Allegheny Cemetery,
Pittsburgh, Pennsylvania

JAMES
MCFARLANE

MILITIA COMMANDER,
REVOLUTIONARY WAR VETERAN

CA. 1751–1794

Mingo Cemetery,
Finleyville, Pennsylvania

The first white men in the West were subject to the same
physical conditions as the Red man. Living in the continual
damp and shade of the primeval forest, sleeping in part on the
ground or near it, exposed to cold and rain as no succeeding
generation has been exposed, the western pioneer became
remarkably phlegmatic; the blood was cold and slow and the
animal spirits consequently in an habitual state of depression
bordering on melancholy. The influence of strong drink on
these men, as on the savages who craved it so eagerly, was
acceptable and exceedingly exhilarating.

—Archer Butler Hulbert, the *Ohio River*

John Neville's plantation, Bower Hill, just south of Pittsburgh, would
have been an impressive sight to neighbors. At sixty years old, he was
appointed revenue collector for four counties in Western Pennsylvania,
a job that would earn him a complicated place in history, since Neville
was a distiller himself.

He was a military man and knew the West well. He had skir-
mished in Washington's command under General Braddock during the
Seven Years' War and had taken Pittsburgh during the Revolutionary War
as a militiaman; he then joined the Continental Army, enduring the winter
at Valley Forge, and fought in several key battles, including Yorktown. By
war's end he was a brigadier general and had been granted land to settle.

Bower Hill was a ten-thousand-acre operation with fields,
outbuildings, barns, and slaves. The two-story home stood out for having clapboard siding, plastered walls and ceilings, and wood floors.

Wallpaper and carpets were among the luxuries enjoyed by Neville and his wife, Winifred. Their son, Presley, lived in a brick house down the hill. Other relatives and in-laws held prominent positions in town, and the family business was supplying the military with goods, including whiskey, as it set off on routine missions down the Ohio River into Indian country.

Neville's plantation stood in stark contrast to his neighbors in the woods of the West, mostly subsistence farmers living in log cabins in the hills and hollows of the Appalachians. To them, Neville represented a kind of eastern elitism they had moved west to avoid.

Back in Philadelphia, Washington worked with his Treasury secretary Alexander Hamilton, a financially savvy politician, to design a tax on distilled spirits to help pay down the war debt. It was also a move to assess a form of taxation in a young nation very opposed to the idea of taxes and duties. Liquor, Hamilton figured, was a luxury, consumed in large quantities in the States, and its production could be organized in a structured way so as to make the tax on producers a routine part of business, and an industrialized distilling trade would function as a revenue arm of the government.

Interestingly, about this time, England banned stills of less than five-hundred-gallon capacity, in effect outlawing the farm distiller and encouraging a commercial scale that could be monitored and taxed with some authority. (If such a tax were enacted today, it would eliminate all but about 5 percent of commercial distilleries and nearly all of the craft distilleries.) Hamilton was watching the English laws from afar and looked to apply the same general principles to an American taxation system. However, though there were plenty of large commercial distilleries in the United States, Hamilton knew he couldn't ban small-scale distillation without alienating the West, where whiskey was understood to be an extension of agricultural life.

Hamilton devised his law to distinguish between town stills and country stills. The stills set up in cities and towns, which could be monitored, would play a flat tax on volume produced. The country stills, which couldn't be easily monitored, would pay a tax on the size of the still. Large distillers paid nine cents for every gallon, and eighty-eight cents for every ten gallons, a graduated rate that offered savings if production was large. Hamilton based the system off his observations of the urban distilleries that employed one-hundred-gallon stills or larger and ran them daily during a four-month distilling season.

Hamilton's math didn't work for the rural stills, which ran less often and for shorter seasons. Additionally, the tax was due in cash, a significant hardship for the frontier farmer who subsisted mostly on barter. In Western Pennsylvania, whiskey *was* cash.

Hamilton sent excise inspectors a manual, hydrometers, and certificates they could use to record still capacity and barrels filled, and to gauge the proof of whiskey stored. The inspector was to keep a ledger, and taxed barrels earned a certificate, almost like a deed, so that buyers knew they were getting registered liquor. Neville received an annual salary of $450 plus a 1-percent commission.

Neville's first hire, Robert Johnson, was to be a deputy in charge of the business. He set about his unpopular task. On a September night in 1791, he encountered a group of twenty men made up in blackface and wearing women's dresses who were carrying muskets and other weapons. They forced Johnson to undress and applied hot tar to his bare skin. They then threw bushels of poultry feathers on his body, cursed at him, took his horse, and fled. Johnson, covered in rapidly hardening pitch, was left alone in the dark with second-degree burns, scarred for the rest of his days.

Over the next two years, unrest grew to a fever pitch in the forks of the Ohio River region. By 1794, barns were burned merely because distillers had agreed to be registered. A straw effigy of Neville was burned, to the delight of a rowdy crowd. A man tried to attack Neville, his wife, and granddaughter on the road, but Neville was able to wrestle him to the ground and throttle him until he yielded. Liberty poles, once symbols of revolution, now were symbols of rebellion: hoisted with the image of a snake on a banner with the phrase "Don't tread on me."

In July 1794, Federal Marshal David Lenox was sent in to serve subpoenas on delinquent distillers. On the fourteenth, Neville and Lenox served William Miller with a fine and a court appearance in Philadelphia. Miller, a war veteran and an honest man, cursed the paperwork, and saw his dreams of a move to Kentucky rapidly fading. Meanwhile, a posse of men gathered in the distance. Shots rang out and Neville, not wanting to engage, was determined to return to his mansion, which had been fortified in anticipation of a siege.

The men rounded up reinforcements and marched to Bower Hill, hoping to take Lenox captive. In the early morning, they found Bower Hill's windows covered with planks. Neville told the men to stand down, then fired into the crowd, mortally wounding Miller's nephew. The rebels fired back, forming a line and serving volleys of musket balls into the house. Winifred reloaded Neville's guns when necessary, and by picking off rebels from a protected vantage point, Neville wounded four more. Neville's young granddaughter lay on the parlor floor to avoid flying musket balls.

The next day a group of soldiers from Fort Pitt, under Major Abraham Kirkpatrick (Winifred's brother-in-law), took up positions in Bower Hill. Neville himself hid in a nearby ravine. The rebels, under the name the Mingo Creek Militia, elected James McFarlane as their leader, and took up battle lines below the house.

Women and children were allowed to leave, and shooting commenced. At one point, the rebels saw what they thought was a white flag waving from a window. McFarlane stepped from behind a tree to tell his men to hold fire. At that lull in the action, a shot rang out from the house, and McFarlane fell dead. The rebels were incensed. They burned the house, captured Kirkpatrick, Presley Neville, and Lenox, but each managed to escape that evening.

Still, the conflict succeeded at escalating the fight over Hamilton's excise tax. With men killed, the Mingo Creek Militia rallied against Washington and earned sympathy on the frontier. Facing a crisis, Washington called up a militia of thirteen thousand men, and led troops for some of the march to Pittsburgh. It was such a serious show of force that the Mingo Creek Militia backed off and a crisis was mostly averted. But still, McFarlane was given a hero's funeral, and the excise tax was repealed seven years later. Neville moved in with his son, a short distance away from his original home. The house still stands and can be visited today. The site of Bower Hill is the parking lot to a Catholic church.

A child of a distiller, in the neigh horhood of Easton, by the name of Potts, had been amusing itself in the distillery while its father was engaged in his labor, and when he was compelled to leave the house for a few moments to bring in a supply of fuel, in playing about a large boiler of swill, by some accident fell into it It was not missed, until half an hour after, when the par nt went to stir the swill, and found his infant a lump of boiled flesh. The feelings of the agonized parent must have been of the most horrid and distressing kind.

Child of Potts
THE *GETTYSBURG COMPILER*,
AUGUST 9, 1826

A TOUR OF SOUTHWESTERN PENNSYLVANIA

THE AREA AROUND PITTSBURGH is home to the early history of whiskey in the United States, especially the Whiskey Rebellion, which lasted for two years and culminated with George Washington's calling in the militia to enforce the position of the federal government. Several rye whiskey distilleries were also located in the region.

1. WHISKEY POINT
Whiskey Rebels gathered here to resolve their grievances

2. JAMES MCFARLANE
Leader of the Whiskey Rebels, shot at Bower Hill, is buried in Mingo Cemetery near Fayetteville

3. WOODVILLE PLANTATION
Site of Presley Neville's house, his father would move in after the Battle of Bower HIll and build this home, which still stands and is open to visitors

4. BOWER HILL
Site of critical siege on John Neville's house in 1794, flash point of Whiskey Rebellion

5. WIGLE WHISKEY
A modern craft distillery is here in downtown Pittsburgh, named after Phillip Wigle, one of two Whiskey Rebels to be convicted. Washington later pardoned him

6. JOHN NEVILLE
Loathed tax collector and nemesis of Whiskey Rebels is buried in Allegheny Cemetery in Pittsburgh

7. HENRY CLAY FRICK
Distiller and industrialist is buried in Homewood Cemetery

8. BRADDOCK'S FIELD
About 6,000 protesters gathered here to argue for secession and plot a raid on Pittsburgh

9. POSSUM HOLLOW DISTILLERY
Possum Hollow was a successful pre-Prohibition brand of rye whiskey, based in McKeesport

10. JOHNSTOWN FLOOD
A short drive will take you to Johnstown Flood National Memorial, where the dam at Henry Clay Frick's private hunting club failed in 1889 and killed 2,209 people

11. WEST OVERTON DISTILLERY
Abraham Overholt built his first modern distillery at this site, also the family farm

12. OLD OVERHOLT DISTILLERY
Site of modern distillery, now defunct, at Broad Ford

13. FORT NECESSITY
Washington's only surrender came when his troops were out of provisions and had only whiskey

HEZEKIAH PIERREPONT

DISTILLER, OWNER OF ANCHOR GIN

1768–1838

———

Green-Wood Cemetery, Brooklyn, New York

Hezekiah Beers Pierrepont invented two things: American gin and the American suburb.

Born in New Haven, he dropped out of college (he was uninterested in the study of Greek and Latin) and made his way to New York City, working for a time in the customshouse. His shipping firm, Leffingwell and Pierrepont, fared well in trading with France during the revolution, where supplies were often thin, until the capture of his ship, the *Confederacy,* by French pirates in 1797.

He lived off and on in Paris for seven years, witnessing the public guillotining of several French revolutionaries, before moving back to New York in 1800. Two years later he married Anna Maria Constable, the largest owner of "wild land in New York." Seeking to settle down, perhaps, and disenchanted with international trade, he engaged Colonel James Anderson (of Connecticut; not to be confused with his contemporary James Anderson of Mount Vernon) to build a distillery for him at the old Livingston distillery, which had burned at some point, probably near the end of the Revolutionary War.

Pierrepont's Anchor Gin, as it was branded, was renowned for its smoothness, having been aged a full year in the distillery's warehouses. He improved the distillery's remaining structures and built a windmill on the dock to power the grain mill. Pierrepont's success was also his downfall: After fifteen years in business, his product was so widely copied that the distillery was no longer profitable and the buildings were sold and converted to candle making. Later owners, including the concern Schenck & Rutherford, used the site to distill rum well into the mid-1800s.

In his time, Pierrepont bought up some of the larger old estates of Brooklyn and moved into a mansion built on Columbia Street, overlooking New York Harbor from the vantage point of Brooklyn Heights. Pierrepont's style was described as "substantial, but modest elegance." Over his mantel hung a painting of George Washington, which can be found today in the Crystal Bridges Museum of Art in Arkansas. He befriended Robert Fulton in Europe and helped him establish steam-powered ferry service between Manhattan and Brooklyn. (They were close enough that Pierrepont named one of his sons Robert Fulton Pierrepont.) Through his investments with Robert Fulton, Pierrepont helped to turn Brooklyn into America's first suburb, incorporating the town in 1815. He laid out a grid of wide streets, which appealed to wealthy bankers and merchants who could use Fulton's regular ferry service to avoid the densely packed, dirty streets of Manhattan.

Pierrepont's son Henry Evelyn would assist in the development of the borough, siting the town's city hall (now Borough Hall) on a triangle of unused land. Henry had studied cities in Europe and applied some of what he had learned to the development of the young town. Henry would also be instrumental in the founding of Green-Wood, New York City's rural cemetery, in 1838, and Hezekiah has a prominent burial there on top of a high knoll, their funerary pavilion designed by Richard Upjohn, who is best known for designing Trinity Church and for founding the American Institute of Architects.

ELIJAH CRAIG

TOBACCO FARMER, MINISTER, ENTREPRENEUR

CA. 1743–1808

Georgetown, Kentucky

E lijah Craig was certainly not the inventor of bourbon, as was often once claimed, but he was an industrious frontier farmer, minister, textile maker, and distiller.

Born to Toliver and Mary Craig in Orange County, Virginia, he began his ministry in 1766 in a tobacco barn in Virginia. He and his two brothers were significant early Baptists, and he was jailed at least once in Culpeper for preaching against the doctrine of the state-sponsored Anglican Church. "He preached to people through the grates during his imprisonment," wrote John H. Spencer, in his history of Baptists in Kentucky. One of Craig's lawyers warned the court that he should be discharged, as his followers were "like a bed of chamomile, the more they are trodden, the more they spread." He had a melodic voice and looked "as a man who had just come from the dead," Spencer wrote. He frequently brought his congregants to tears.

Craig moved to Kentucky in 1786 and took to frontier life. "The temptation was too strong," Spencer wrote. "He was soon overwhelmed by worldly business . . . [he] vainly imagined he could serve God and mammon both." He founded the Kentucky town of Georgetown, where he built a gristmill, ropewalk, fulling mill, and paper mill. The paper mill was what Lewis Collins, in his history of Kentucky from 1882, spends the most time describing; a two-and-a-half-story structure about forty by sixty feet with a large iron screw, presumably part of the papermaking machinery, imported from England. Collins also suggests the first bourbon whiskey was distilled at the same site in 1789, leaving later readers to suspect Craig. Nearly all of the accounts of Craig's distilling life appear seventy years after his death, so their credibility is questionable.

It's possible, even probable, that distilling occurred near the mill around 1790, as Collins suggests, but there were other distillers in Kentucky at that time and it could have been that Craig supplied capital or property, but may not have been distilling. Historian Henry Crowgey points out that a prominent Kentucky distiller, Lewis Sanders, once eulogized Craig in 1827, but made no mention of his distilling. Craig was fined in 1798 for making whiskey without a license, but two hundred others in Kentucky were also fined that year.

The modern-day brand of bourbon is distilled at Bernheim distillery in Louisville and ages in warehouses near Heaven Hill's headquarters in Bardstown, Kentucky. The company does not trace any direct relationship to Craig, but as a start-up after Prohibition, the name seemed as good as any (its other flagship bourbon, Evan Williams, is named after Kentucky's first distiller, a title that is easily refuted).

A nineteenth-century revival, like the one at Cane Ridge Revival where Craig preached

RICHARD SEAVY

DISTILLER

1811–1841

Interment unknown

An Irish immigrant named Richard Seavy, age thirty, was burned and scalded at the Scribner & Hitchcock distillery September 9th, 1841 on Manhattan's Lower East Side. "While drawing liquor from the receiving box into hogsheads," wrote the *Evening Post,* "some of the liquor splashed out." Some of the spirit splashed on a lamp, whereupon the flame traveled to the receiving box, setting the clothes of Seavy and another man on fire. Seavy "wrapped in flames, ran out and jumped into a kettle of boiling water to extinguish the flames, from which he was taken out, partly burnt and partly scalded, and died at 4½ o'clock yesterday morning."

ANDREW JACKSON

GENERAL, PRESIDENT, DISTILLER

1767–1845

The Hermitage, Davidson County, Tennessee

V ery little has been written about Jackson as a distiller, but it is known that a still operated at the Hermitage, his home in Nashville, and before that at his Hunter's Hill Farm. His familiarity with whiskey, both as a maker and a consumer, surely bolstered his image as a leader of the common man.

Jackson grew up in North Carolina, and during the Revolutionary War served as a courier, for which he was captured and starved. His brothers died in the war; his mother died while nursing sick American prisoners on a ship in Charleston—all the makings of a grudge that would give Jackson great satisfaction in avenging, famously, at the Battle of New Orleans. Jackson studied law in North Carolina and then moved to the territory that would become Tennessee, where his scrappy character was well suited to succeed as a lawyer and then a judge, while managing a plantation and his distillery.

In 1799, Jackson obtained a license to work two stills, one 127-gallon and one 70-gallon pot. In 1800, the distillery burned: "All his cooper ware and his Stills rendered entirely unfit for use inasmuch as the caps and worms were almost entirely destroyed by the heat and the

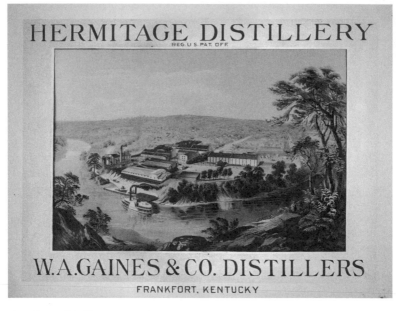

Hermitage Distillery

falling in of the roof and timber," Thomas Hutchings wrote in a deposition as part of a petition for tax leniency after the fire. Also lost were three hundred gallons of whiskey. Jackson wrote several letters trying to clear up his tax obligation on the destroyed stills, though the tax would be repealed shortly after the incident by Thomas Jefferson's administration. Jackson owned slaves, as many as forty-four at one point, though how many worked in the distillery is unknown. Receipts from Jackson's rebuilt distillery in 1802 reference a business partner, Thomas Watson, and show corn, rye, firewood, four tight barrels, as well as a payment to William Irby for "setting the stills," perhaps evidence that he was Jackson's distiller.

As a young man in Tennessee, Jackson was known as a gambler, betting on billiards, cards, cockfights, and, of course, racehorses, including Truxton, a stallion fifteen hands, three inches high, bought for fifteen hundred dollars on a special trip to Virginia to find a breeding horse. He was known to drink, "occasionally hilarious over his whiskey and wine," wrote James Parton, an early biographer.

In 1804, Jackson moved to the Hermitage, a Greek Revival plantation that would serve as the home he would make with Rachel Donelson, whose previous marriage would end up causing Jackson some grief in his successful campaign for president in 1828. Rachel had "lustrous black eyes, dark glossy hair, full red lips, brunette complexion, though of brilliant coloring, [and] a sweet oval face rippling with smiles and dimples," wrote the daughter of a niece, which is to say that she must have been quite beautiful in her time. Jackson doted on her and had to be pulled away when she died suddenly just days before he was to begin his term as president. Her niece would serve as the First Lady, a role that has on occasion fell to non-spousal relatives.

Jackson no doubt served and consumed much whiskey while at the White House, where he presided over one of the ugliest presidencies in history. Even after his death in 1845, Jackson proved to be an irresistible marketing image for the whiskey industry: Both Old Hickory and Hermitage were popular brands over the next century.

WILLIAM HENRY HARRISON

GENERAL, PRESIDENT, DISTILLER

1773–1841

William Henry Harrison Memorial, North Bend, Ohio

William Henry Harrison is the third of our dead "General, President, Distillers," a surprisingly common string of titles for early chief executives. Harrison is mostly known to history by a single fact: At his inaugural address in 1841, he caught pneumonia and died thirty-two days later. He remains the shortest-serving president in American history.

Harrison's father, Benjamin Harrison V, a patriot and founding father, was a notorious imbiber. He was a large man, and joked at the signing of the Declaration of Independence that "I shall have a great advantage over you, Mr. Gerry, when we are all hung for what we are now doing. From the size and weight of my body I shall die in a few minutes, but from the lightness of your body, you will dance in the air an hour or two before you are dead." John Adams called him Falstaff, after the jovial, somewhat sad Shakespearean figure. He died at a celebration at the Berkeley plantation on the James River, where another dead distiller, George Thorpe (see page 24), met his fate in an Indian raid.

Benjamin hoped his son would enter medical school, but after his father's death, young William joined the army. He married Anna Tuthill Symmes against her father's wishes, eloping and honeymooning at the military installation at Fort Washington in Cincinnati. After successful military service, he became a congressional representative and eventually governor of the Indiana Territory. Harrison was a shrewd manager and, like Andrew Jackson before him, worked to expand territory at the expense of American Indians. He won political support by giving away whiskey and cider at election times, and he was similarly generous to the Indians when he hoped to weaken them. He won a minor but psychologically important victory at the Battle of Tippecanoe and earned his nickname from the river where the battle was fought. Later, he commanded a successful fight against the British at the Battle of the Thames during the War of 1812.

After his military career ended, and after years of holding government posts, he returned to Ohio and set about building a commercial farm. Samuel Jones Burr wrote, "His farm on the Ohio River contains very superior corn ground, and some years since, when corn was low, he established a distillery in order to convert his surplus into an article more portable and profitable." Harrison wasn't the only person to have this idea; in fact, one of the distilleries established in Harrison's time, first known as the Dunn and Ludlow distillery, remains today as the MGP distillery in Lawrenceburg, just five miles east from where Harrison is buried in North Bend, Ohio. Harrison also ran a successful horse-breeding business.

Harrison didn't like to drink, even though his political campaign liked to portray him as a cabin-dwelling cider drinker. One of his sons struggled with alcoholism. Harrison shuttered his distillery. In June 1831, with his eye on national politics, he publicly declared his opposition to alcohol and gave this speech to the Hamilton County Agricultural Society in June 1831:

> The exports of Ohio are generally the substantial comforts of life, which are everywhere acceptable, their arrival hailed as a blessing as well in the mansions of the rich as in the cottage of the poor; by the luxurious inhabitant of the tropics, cloyed with the luscious product of his burning climate, as by the poor negro who ministers to his wants. Alas! that there should be an *exception*; that a soil so prolific for that which is good, should, by a perversion of the intentions of the Creator, be made to yield that which is evil to scatter life and death with an equal hand. To the heart cheering prospects of flocks and herds feeding on unrivalled pastures of grain, exhibiting the scriptural proof that the seed had been cast on good ground—how often is the eye of the philanthropic traveller disgusted with the dark unsightly manufactories of certain poison—poison to the body and the soul!—A modern

Aeneas or Ulysses might mistake them for entrances into the infernal regions, nor would they greatly err. But unlike those passages which conducted the Grecian and Trojan heroes on their pious errands, the scenes to which all these conduct the unhappy wretch who shall enter them are those, exclusively, of misery and woe. No relief to the sad picture; no Tartarus *there*, no Elysium *here*. It is all Tartarie darkness, and not unfrequently Tartarie crime.

I speak more freely of the practice of converting the material of "the staff of life" (and for which so many human beings yearly perish) into an article which is so destructive of health and happiness, because in that way I have sinned myself; but in that way I shall sin no more.

William Henry Harrison, for his thirty-two days on the presidential stage, endures in history: erstwhile whiskey distiller, reformed; temperance advocate; Indian killer. But perhaps his most lasting contribution to history is his political campaign. Recast as a rube by Democrat Martin Van Buren and eastern newspapers, Harrison and his party turned this to his advantage, creating all kinds of propaganda showing Harrison as a man of the people. The most enduring, a log cabin–shaped bottle of whiskey, was marked by the E. C. Booz company. It proved wildly popular, ensuring that company's legacy, though not, as is often claimed, the word "booze" as a synonym for liquor. (The term actually traces its roots back to a Dutch word, *busen*, meaning excessive drinking.)

THOMAS GLARTHEY

SWILL BOY

1836 OR 1837–1845

Interment unknown

O n February 7th, 1845, Thomas Glarthey was disobeying his father's wishes and hanging around the Cunningham and Harris distillery on the Brooklyn waterfront, a dangerous place where boys were regularly injured. Draymen would line up their carts under a pipe that stuck out over the street, and boys would be sent to stir the swill in the cistern so as not to clog the pipe. Thomas was sent, but unfortunately fell in, suffered severe burns, and died about two hours later.

At the coroner's inquest, an unusual episode was recounted in the *Brooklyn Daily Eagle*, as follows: "An individual who had evidently been indulging in 'libations deep and strong,' and who until then had been unobserved, arose from a corner of the room where he had been dozing, and insisted that the Coroner was premature in holding an Inquisition upon [Glarthey]." The man apparently continued, "he was not yet dead" and offered to drink a glass of brandy if anyone would pay for it to prove his case. According to the *Eagle*, "This did not satisfy the foreman of the Jury—who is somewhat of a wag—and he moved that the Jury declare (informally however) their unanimous opinion that the said personage was dead—drunk."

THOMAS LINCOLN

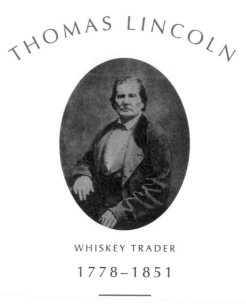

WHISKEY TRADER

1778–1851

Shiloh Cemetery, Pleasant Grove Township, Illinois

Born in Virginia, Thomas Lincoln moved west with his father into Kentucky to a remote plot of frontier land at the suggestion of a distant relative, the pioneer Daniel Boone. At age eight, while he and his two older brothers were planting in a field a good distance from their house, they witnessed their father's attack and murder by an Indian. His older brother, Mordecai, shot the Indian dead with a rifle moments later. His mother, Bathsheba, moved the family again to Nelson County, Kentucky.

Generally unambitious and incompetent, Lincoln rarely found paying jobs in Kentucky, though he was known as a decent carpenter. He married in 1806 and, after a decade of hard luck, endeavored to move north to Indiana, where land was reportedly inexpensive and fertile. When the time came, he traded his worldly goods for whiskey barrels he hoped would serve as the currency for a new life. His two young sons attended the casting off of the boat from the Rolling Fork River into the Ohio, but the boat capsized in an eddy, sending several barrels and a set of tools into the river. Some barrels were recovered, as were the tools, and Lincoln found an oxcart to bring them to the new land where he eventually settled.

One of his sons, young Abraham, would never be much of a drinker, perhaps because he witnessed much of the family fortune floating down the river. In 1862, acting in his capacity as sixteenth president of the United States, he passed into law an emergency wartime revenue act, taxing sinful and luxurious goods such as tobacco, playing cards, pianos, yachts, feathers, and distilled spirits, thus creating in the United States the concept of the illicit distiller, or moonshiner. Lincoln's excise tax, though designed as a stopgap measure to raise funds for the Union, remains to this day, and helped fund expansion of the federal government after the Civil War, until the income tax passed in 1913.

Thomas Lincoln and his son stopped speaking in later years. They disagreed over the virtue of religion and education. The younger Lincoln did not attend his father's funeral and would not pay for a headstone.

THE BROOKLYN *DAILY EAGLE*,

FEBRUARY 19, 1846

ALEXANDER MCNAIR

DREADFUL ACCIDENT—*A boy named Alexander Mc-Nair, aged fourteen years, accidentally fell into a vat of scalding liquor, at the distillery of Gen. Manley, in Tillary Street yesterday afternoon. The poor boy was immediately rescued and conveyed to his home, where he lingered until this morning in the greatest agony, and notwithstanding the exertions of several skillful physicians, then expired. The Coroner will hold an inquest over the body during the course of the day.*

The above vat is described as a dangerous sort of trap, into which several boys have been caught and scalded during the past year. Young McNair had come for and was in the act of procuring swill, when he met with the sad accident above narrated.

JAMES C. CROW

DISTILLER

1789–1856

Versailles Cemetery, Woodford County, Kentucky

James Crow was trained as a physician at the College of Medicine and Surgery in Edinburgh and immigrated to the United States around 1822. First settling in Philadelphia, he went bankrupt and headed west. He arrived in Kentucky around 1825 and found work at the distillery of Colonel Willis Field. His medical training, and subsequent scientific approach to distilling, would have a profound effect on the whiskey business.

In an article in the *New York Times* from 1897, Crow is described as having a "herculean build, broad, intellectual forehead, smooth-shaven face, with the deep blue eyes and sandy complexion charac-teristic of his race." According to the *Times*, distilling at the time of Crow's arrival in Kentucky was done "after the manner of the old negro mammy's formula for bread making, taking 'a passel' of meal, 'a passel' of malt, and about 'so much' water, 'b'iled down' until it was done." Crow's library was described as the most extensive in Kentucky, and his scientific instruments helped him improve—and, crucially, make more reliable—the whiskey-making process. One advancement that Crow likely introduced or perfected is the notion of narrow "cuts." Crow took only two-and-a-half gallons of spirit per bushel (fifty-six pounds dry), whereas most distillers took twice that, suggesting Crow was interested in a narrower, higher-quality fraction of the distilling run.

Crow became the head distiller at the Oscar Pepper distillery, already a well-established concern near Millville, in Woodford County. After twenty years, he went to work at the Johnson distillery just a little ways down Glenn's Creek. He died on the job in 1856 (some sources list 1859).

Crow is sometimes credited with inventing the sour mash pro-cess, in which fermented mash from one batch is used to jump-start the fermentation of the next. This isn't true, but he was certainly responsible

The Oscar Pepper Distillery in 1883

for sanitary improvements, such as moving livestock pens away from the distillery, and innovations in testing the acidity of mashes, which improved performance in replicable processes. And Crow's whiskey earned wide acclaim, commanding significantly higher prices than other whiskeys and reportedly favored by Henry Clay and Daniel Webster (and a host of others, including Hunter S. Thompson, much later).

While the name of the distillery was Oscar Pepper, the whiskey was often called "Old Crow's Whiskey, Oscar Pepper Distillery," in an unusual instance of a whiskey named simultaneously for its maker and provenance. Oscar Pepper died a little after Crow. In his will, Pepper's wife inherited control of the distillery, and she leased it to E. H. Taylor (see page 117). Oscar's son, James Pepper, was keen to go into the distilling business himself, but an economic downturn in the1870s hit the distilling business hard and the Peppers and Taylor both went bankrupt.

The Pepper distillery ended up in the hands of Labrot & Graham, and James Pepper launched a new venture with Crow's acolyte, William Mitchell. Both businesses wanted to use the name Pepper. The court was asked to answer the question: Which was the Oscar Pepper distillery? The site where the elder Pepper had made the whiskey or the family process that James insisted he continued in the new facility? What makes whiskey, the place or the procedure? The law sided with the land, not the blood, and the old Oscar Pepper distillery continues to make whiskey today as Woodford Reserve, just down the road from where old Crow is buried.

CHARLES WILSON	THOMAS GAFF	CHARLES LOUIS FLEISCHMANN
DISTILLER	SHIPPER, DISTILLER	YEAST MAKER, DISTILLER
1798–1858	1808–1884	1835–1897
——	——	——
Green-Wood Cemetery, Brooklyn, New York	*Spring Grove Cemetery, Cincinnati, Ohio*	*Spring Grove Cemetery, Cincinnati, Ohio*

T homas Gaff was born in Scotland and moved with his parents to New Jersey when he was a toddler. Gaff learned the distilling business from an uncle, Charles Wilson, also born in Scotland, whose Brooklyn distillery opened around 1834 and was described as the oldest and largest in Brooklyn by an 1851 survey, consuming 3,360 tons of grain to make 480,000 gallons of whiskey annually, at a spot between Franklin Avenue and Skillman Street. Charles Wilson's distillery was probably the largest in the country at the time, making as much as 2 percent of the whiskey produced in America and close to 17 percent of what was being produced in New York City. The business employed eighteen people and supported eight hundred dairy cows with distillery swill, or spent beer.

Thomas Gaff left his uncle's operation, and briefly opened a distillery in Philadelphia in the 1830s, but when business turned, after the panic of 1837, he moved west and built a new distillery on Hogan Creek in Southern Indiana. His plant, in the town of Aurora, was once part of a string of distilleries that hugged the northern bank of the Ohio River, though now only the MGP distillery remains. (It is in Lawrenceburg, one town upriver from Aurora and not far from the farm in Ohio where William Henry Harrison [see page 54] had run a distillery.)

Gaff made bourbon, rye, and Thistle Dew Scotch-style whiskey (say "Thistle Dew" out loud to get the joke). He and his brother Thomas also helped Charles and Max Fleischmann set up a yeast–cake business in Cincinnati; they subsequently opened their own distillery, making Fleischmann gin and whiskey. Charles's son Julius took over the family business, adding a grain elevator, a malting company, and a vinegar brewery, and he also became president of the Market National Bank. He was a co-owner of a professional baseball team in Cincinnati and owned several racehorses. When he was twenty-eight, he became Cincinnati's youngest mayor, serving from 1900 to 1905. He died of a heart attack while playing polo in 1925. In 1929, his family's yeast business was bought by J. P. Morgan—whose great-uncle Hezekiah Pierrepont (see page 46) is also a dead distiller. A bottom-shelf version of Fleischmann's whiskey still exists today, and the company, now owned by Barton Brands, is one of the few labels to make whiskey, vodka, brandy, and gin under the same name.

As for Gaff, he branched out of the distillery business, with interests in canal construction, mining, public utilities, Louisiana plantations, a jewelry store, breakfast cereal, and a brand of beer considered of such significant quality that it was exported to Germany. He also invested heavily in steamboats, as his position on the Ohio River afforded opportunities for trade downriver, especially with New Orleans. One of his steamboats was used by General Sherman as a headquarters during the Siege of Vicksburg.

His mansion, Hillforest, now a national historic landmark, was designed by architect Isaiah Rogers to echo the maritime architecture of riverboats. Its rooftop belvedere evokes a pilothouse, while its curved portico, thin columns, arched windows, and a flying staircase in the entrance hall all evoke the paddle-wheel steamers so associated with river travel in the nineteenth century.

The Gaffs and Fleischmanns are buried prominently across from each other in Cincinnati's Spring Grove Cemetery, on opposite sides of a small lake. Gaff's tombstone, in pink marble, was a joint expense by three distilling Gaff brothers. The Fleischmann family mausoleum is a white-marble scale replica of the Parthenon.

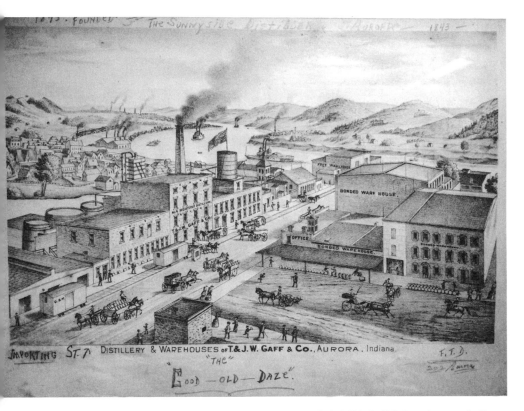

T. & J. W. Gaff & Co., Aurora, Indiana

WILLIAM
P.
SQUIBB

WHISKEY DISTILLER

1831–1913

———

Greendale Cemetery,
near Lawrenceburg, Indiana

EDWARD
R.
SQUIBB

MEDICINAL DISTILLER

1819–1900

———

Green-Wood Cemetery,
Brooklyn, New York

There are two Squibbs that became known for distilling, both descended from Nathaniel Squibb, who lived through the Revolutionary War in Pennsylvania. Nathaniel had two sons, Robert and Enoch Robert. Robert stayed in the northeast, and Nathaniel's grandson, Edward R. Squibb, went to medical school and ran the hospital in the Brooklyn Navy Yard. There, he was the first to employ a steam coil, rather than a direct flame, when distilling medicinal ether. In 1858, he left the military and began making his own medicines in a lab on the Brooklyn waterfront. Later, he created a compact medicine chest to treat battlefield victims during the Civil War.

Rather than patenting his medical improvements, he published the technology so that society might benefit from his ideas and practical improvements. His experimentation, if methodical, was also volatile, and his Brooklyn laboratory often exploded; he was badly burned by one episode. His company exists today as Bristol-Myers Squibb.

Nathaniel's son Enoch Robert moved to the frontier in Indiana. Nathaniel's grandsons, William and George, entered the whiskey business in 1846 as rectifiers and in 1867 built their own distillery with a capacity of three hundred bushels per day (about nine hundred gallons). Business went well, making Chimney Corner, Old Dearborn, Rock Castle, and Gold Leaf rye. In 1885, a continuous still was added.

In 1913, both William and George died, and their sons rebuilt the distillery to a capacity of three thousand gallons a day. But Prohibition advocates had been circling, and the expansion proved ill-fated.

Prohibition should not have been a surprise to the Squibbs: William was constantly facing lawsuits and complaints about his feeding cattle distillery swill, or selling milk from cattle fed on distillery by-products, a common complaint against distillers from temperance advocates. (During the war, William's son Nathaniel had testified as to the feed value of distillation by-products at a time when nationalistic sentiment, calls to ration grain, and temperance advocacy seemed to fuse in an unholy political marriage.)

With the state of Indiana enacting its own Prohibition in 1917, the Squibb distillery closed. It would later be acquired by George Remus (see page 155) and Lew Rosenstiel (see page 213). The distillery today is abandoned, on a site just north of MGP Ingredients, which makes bulk whiskey for private bottlers, including Bulleit, Templeton, Redemption, and others.

A TOUR OF GREEN-WOOD CEMETERY

Green-Wood Cemetery is located in Brooklyn's Sunset Park, not far from the Frederick Law Olmsted-designed Prospect Park, though Green-Wood predates that park by thirty years. Once a popular tourist destination, second only to Niagara Falls, the cemetery is now a place of surprising quietude in the otherwise bustling City of New York.

1. HEZEKIAH PIERREPONT
Distiller of Anchor Gin, founding family of Green-Wood Cemetery, friend of Robert Fulton, suburb inventor

2. SAMUEL MORSE
Inventor of the telegraph

3. E. R. SQUIBB
Medicinal distiller, improver of distillation technology, founder of Bristol-Myers Squibb

4. BOSS TWEED
Political strategist

5. CHARLES WILSON
Prominent Brooklyn distiller making half a million gallons annually in 1850, mentor to Thomas Gaff

6. CLINTON GILBERT
Civil War veteran, revenue officer, gauger, shot in the groin in the line of duty, only casualty of Brooklyn Whiskey Wars

7. GENERAL JAMES JOURDAN
Commanding officer during Whiskey Raids, personally attended Clinton Gilbert's injuries in 1871

8. BATTLE HILL
Highest point in Brooklyn, site of most successful American military activity in Battle of Brooklyn

9. RICHARD HAYES MACDONALD
Kentuckian, president of the Bank of California, teetotaller

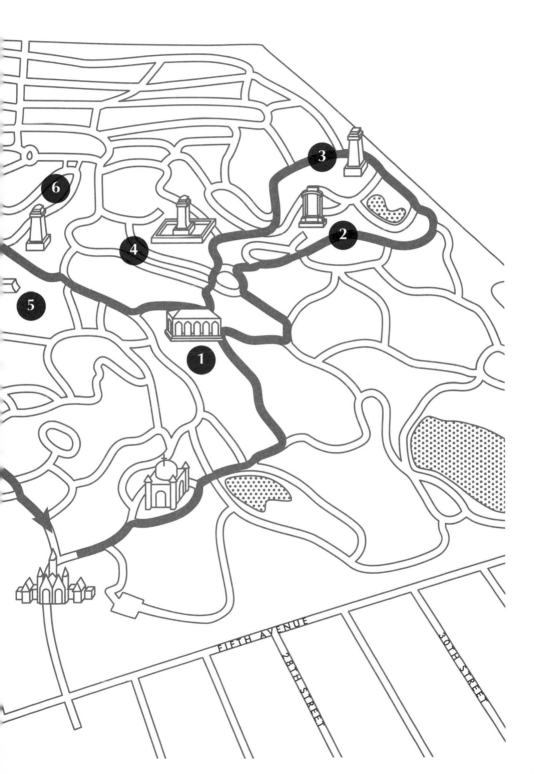

RAID ON ILLICIT WHISKY STILLS IN BROOKLYN.—[Sketched by Theo. R. Davis.]

CLINTON GILBERT

GAUGER

1846–1871

Green-Wood Cemetery, Brooklyn, New York

I n 1871, the great Whiskey Wars of Brooklyn were coming to a head. For several months, the federal government, in order to enforce unpopular laws taxing whiskey production, was sending raids of hundreds and sometimes more than a thousand troops into the Irish neighborhood adjacent to the docks in Brooklyn, then called Irishtown, where many distillers were making illegal whiskey. At the end of the Civil War, an expansion of federal powers had required additional revenue, which was meant to come from whiskey tax, a burden that was viewed as unfairly targeted at Brooklyn Democrats, many of them Irish immigrants.

General James Jourdan, assessor for the revenue district, working in the same position as Alfred Pleasonton, who was now commissioner of the entire revenue service, knew his boss was aware of the difficulty of Brooklyn's Fifth Ward. Months of raids had yielded no results; the illicit distilleries were merely rebuilt, and it was feared that without arrests, the illegal moonshining would go on indefinitely.

The hope was to arrest four men: John Bridges, J. H. Cassidy, Michael McMahon, and John Gorman. Gorman's still was known to the revenue office; they'd destroyed it a year prior but found he had rebuilt it and was continuing to flout the law. And with the passage of the 1870 Enforcement Act, designed to handle the Ku Klux Klan in the South, the government was authorized to use federal troops to enforce reconstruction policies, one of which was the protection of revenue. In the early morning on July 14, 1871, a group of fifty soldiers assisted forty revenue agents as they split up to serve the arrest warrants at the suspected distilleries. They left the gate of the Brooklyn Navy Yard at two A.M., and, under cover of darkness, hoped to catch the moonshiners at work.

By the time the officers showed up at Gorman's distillery, he was gone, the bricks still hot from where the still had been heating. Bridges was nowhere to be found. McMahon was arrested, though he jumped from a second-story window in his undershirt and fled through several adjoining sheds before being confronted with a pistol.

In the worst part of the moonshine district, on the way to Cassidy's residence on a short street known as Dickson's Alley, Jourdan and his men were proceeding with caution. At the corner of York and Hudson, just as the dozen or so men accompanying him passed under a streetlamp, a shot rang out. Firing back, the marines sent a volley of pistol fire into the dark, but the assailants were crouched down and well hidden. Men on both sides were struck by bullets, and the fighting continued for a few minutes until the moonshiners abandoned their fight and fled toward the river. The officers proceeded to Cassidy's, and he submitted.

When the smoke cleared, Clinton Gilbert, age twenty-five, a gauger (an official tasked with determining the proof of spirits by means of a Treasury department hydrometer), had been shot through the groin, his injuries severe. Captain Selvage was shot in the ankle, and a bullet hit Major Weeks in the hand. Gilbert staggered back into the yard, and eventually to the Naval Hospital, where he died the following day. He was given a hero's funeral, attended by a large delegation of fellow veterans of the Civil War, at the Washington Avenue Baptist Church.

After Gilbert's murder, the distillers of Brooklyn earned a reputation that we might associate with drug dealers today, perhaps summarized best by a government functionary writing under the pen name Franklin Eliot Felton, in his book *The Secrets of Internal Revenue*:

> The production of whiskey from cereals requires larger capital, greater space, more extensive buildings, a higher degree of skill, and more complete machinery and apparatus than the manufacture of Molasses Whiskey, and the contraband distillers of Grain Whiskey constitute an aristocracy of malefactors. They reside in well-furnished houses belonging to themselves, drive fast horses and fancy wagons, patronize the races in

which they enter their crack nags, frequent the barrooms of
the most fashionable hotels, where they pass their leisure time
in conversing about their illegal traffic, discussing the work-
ings and changes of the Revenue law, devising new schemes
to defraud the government, and criticizing the operations and
improvements of the plans already adopted. They are men of
limited education and vulgar manners, which they endeavor
to conceal by aping the address of respectable business men.
They assume an owl-like reticence to impress their associates
with their caution, vigilance and reserve, which qualities are
esteemed to be the highest virtues in persons pursuing their
nefarious and clandestine avocation.

Gilbert's hospital admission form

tous in that jurisdiction, and small bands of Spaniards and Cubans are engaged in mutual murder and robbery."

Illicit Distilleries in the South —Shooting, &c.

MEMPHIS, May 24—12:45 P. M.

On Saturday night an armed band of disguised men stopped the train from Louisville to Memphis, and attempted to murder Internal Revenue Officer Hahn, who had a prisoner on board, arrested for running an illicit distilley. Hahn's assistant, name unknown, jumped from the train, was fired on by the band, and was seen to fall.

Mr. Hahn fired into the gang, killing one of them. The others poured a volley into the train, fortunately without injuring any one. The train was immediately put in motion. The last seen of the band they were making for the woods, bearing their comrade. The band is susposed to belong to a gang engaged in illicit distilleries extending from East Tennessee to Mississippi.

Instructions to Minister Motley.

WASHINGTON, May 23.—The most that can be reliably ascertainéd of the instructions to Minister Motley is that

Internal Revenue Officer Hahn's
Assistant and Unnamed Moonshiner
THE *HIGHLAND WEEKLY NEWS*
(HILLSBORO, OHIO), MAY 27, 1869

OHIO.

Accidents at Dayton — Unfortunate Quarrel at Mansfield.

DAYTON, August 8.—A man named Anderson, employed in Harris' distillery, fell into a mash-tub this morning, and was horribly scalded. He will probably die.

A little boy, five years old, was drowned this morning in the canal.

Councilman Barnhart, shot Saturday, is better to-day, and will probably recover.

The subscription for the new Music Hall has been nearly all taken.

Captain Thomas J. Barry
THE *INDIANAPOLIS NEWS*,
AUGUST 9, 1870

ORVILLE ELIAS BABCOCK

PRIVATE SECRETARY TO ULYSSES S. GRANT,
WHISKEY RINGLEADER

1835–1884

Arlington National Cemetery, Arlington, Virginia

Orville Elias Babcock graduated third in his class from West Point in 1861, just in time to start fighting in the Civil War. He first worked to fortify Washington, D.C., against attack, then helped build a strategic pontoon bridge at Harpers Ferry. After proving himself as an engineer, he moved around the country in various roles and theaters, eventually becoming General Ulysses Grant's top aide.

After the war, he resigned his commission, and when Grant became president he acted as his personal secretary and advisor. In 1869, Grant sent Babcock on a secret mission to Santo Domingo, with an unusual plan to annex the Dominican Republic (then known as Santo Domingo) and create a "Negro state" there, or at least alleviate some tension between blacks and whites during Reconstruction by offering territory in an American protectorate. The plan failed.

Soon after, Babcock became embroiled in a scandal in which a group of revenue agents, working with distillers, rectifiers, gaugers, and functionaries in the revenue and Treasury department, bribed and stole millions of dollars from the federal government. The idea was to pay less tax on whiskey produced, which they achieved through a variety of means including labeling whiskey as vinegar, falsifying proof statements, and running the distilleries illegally at night. Five men in the revenue office were the ringleaders, pocketing the cash and creating a political slush fund for western Republicans. Distilleries that refused to participate were slapped with fines and penalties for minor infractions of production regulations. Babcock seems to have been a willing participant. According to the historian Peter Krass, his "immoderate appetites for clothing, drink, and fornication—all to be satisfied at the cost of the public treasury—led him to ever more brazen adventures and needless risks." Babcock wore a diamond shirt stud worth twenty-four hundred dollars, and one imagines he might not have been able to afford it on a White House administrative salary.

Only when Benjamin Bristow was appointed secretary of the Treasury, and worked with secret agents and Attorney General Edward Pierrepont (a cousin of Hezekiah's; see page 46), was the ring exposed. Bristow, a Kentuckian, would later say only one-third of the tax due would actually make its way to the U.S. Treasury; this at a time when alcohol tax made more than 50 percent of the federal revenue. President Grant was willing to testify in Babcock's defense (though in the end he merely gave a deposition), and Babcock was exonerated. In 1876, Babcock was indicted again in a complicated case where a group of contractors, on trial for graft, used dynamite to fake a burglary in the safe of a district attorney and then planted documents supposedly taken from the safe in the home of Columbus Alexander, a witness for the prosecution against the contractors and a critic of the Grant administration. The ruse fell apart when the hired burglars turned against the contractors and Babcock was again implicated. His involvement wasn't proven, but by now Grant had to get him out of the White House.

After the scandal, Babcock went back to the Army Corps of Engineers and was sent to help finish construction on the Mosquito Inlet Lighthouse, near Daytona Beach. When he arrived, the boat that was to bring him to the site capsized, and Babcock drowned. He and his boat mates were found onshore, buried in sand, their legs bitten off by sharks.

MOONSHINER

UNKNOWN, ACTIVE 1886

Interment unknown

In the late nineteenth century, the production of distilled apple cider—known variously as applejack, Jersey lightning, and apple whiskey—was growing in New Jersey, then and perhaps still the largest producer of apple-based illegal distillate in the country. In those days, applejack cost about one dollar a gallon for new-make spirit, though aged versions commanded up to three dollars.

A *Brooklyn Daily Eagle* article from 1896 references a moonshine distiller who, ten years earlier, operated on a "wholesale" scale. Investigators fixated on a character "of a lightweight mentally" who was known around Warren County as Crazy Nancy. She lived in the mountains, harvesting wild berries in the summer and hunting small animals for pelts to sell in winter. Nancy was a mysterious woman and didn't enjoy interacting much with strangers, other than to sell them something. She lived in an old barn originally built to house sheep, up against a bluff so as to be out of the wind. Suspicion primarily came from apple farmers in the Pequest River Valley worried about their disappearing crop; despite setting various traps, they were unable to catch the thieves that might be supplying the moonshine trade.

A detective named Finch was assigned to the case. Finch worked for a neighbor by day and stole away in the evenings to watch over Nancy's property. One evening, safely hidden behind some shrubbery, Finch witnessed a man approach Nancy's house with a sack of apples slung over his back. Finch waited but did not see the man again that evening.

Finch, being both fearless and hubristic, decided to pursue the case on his own. He packed a pistol and headed toward Nancy's place. Ascertaining that no one was home, he picked the lock and entered. Nancy's house was sparsely furnished, and the only signs of life were a string of dried apples and a few pumpkins. A ladder led to a loft area with only a flour barrel in the corner. Deciding to lay low, he hid himself behind the barrel and waited for Nancy or the man to return. Eventually, Nancy arrived and cooked her supper by the fire. Finch waited upstairs. When Nancy had finished cooking, she came up to the loft, just steps away from where Finch waited. He saw her remove some boards from the wall, revealing a secret tunnel into the hillside. Nancy disappeared into a door at the end of the tunnel. A half hour later, a man emerged from the door, and only when he came into the loft with a lit candle did Finch realize it was Nancy in men's clothing. She exited the house and Finch maintained his position, hoping to ambush her with a full sack of contraband.

As soon as Nancy was gone, Finch removed the wallboards and snuck into the cave, finding fifty jugs, a barrel of apples, and a full moonshining setup, along with a pile of women's clothing. Finch went downstairs to wait for Nancy.

Around midnight, she arrived in her disguise, and, upon entering the house, lit a candle. Just when she was going to stoke the fire, Finch leveled his pistol at Nancy's back, and said, "Hold up your hands." Nancy whipped around and blew out the candle. Finch, flailing in the darkness, fired his pistol, only to feel the smack of a stool being thrown in his face. As Finch reeled, Nancy ran out the open door and disappeared, never to be seen in Warren County again.

Officials searched the property and found five hundred gallons of applejack hidden throughout the house and in the hillside cave. It was speculated that she hid her jugs in buckets of chestnuts and sold her wares in New York and Philadelphia.

JOSEPH
WASHINGTON
DANT

MINOR
CASE
BEAM

THOMAS
JEFFERSON
POTTINGER

DISTILLER

DISTILLER

DISTILLER

1820–1902

1857–1934

1851–1911

———

———

———

*St. Francis of Assisi
Cemetery,
Marion County,
Kentucky*

*Riverview Cemetery,
New Haven, Kentucky*

*Private cemetery located
off Highway 52 near
Gethsemane, Kentucky*

The area west of the Appalachians was supposed to be Indian lands. That agreement held for much of the colonial British period. By 1775, there were only two hundred people living in all of Kentucky, and fewer in Tennessee. After the Revolutionary War, nationalism, pioneerism, disrespect for Indians, and entrepreneurship drove settlers into Kentucky, which was not heavily populated by Indians and treated as a communal hunting ground by several tribes. The eastern part of the state was hilly, with narrow valleys unsuitable to farming. The earliest settlers found the rich bottomland of the Bluegrass region to be more hospitable and settled in the tributaries of the Ohio River that cut into the plateaus and knobs of Northern and Central Kentucky.

Around the same time, some Catholics were leaving Maryland (originally a Catholic haven among the thirteen colonies) and moving as a group to Kentucky. Many settled in what was then Nelson County, eager to take advantage of the rich land of the frontier and forge new lives in proximity with other Catholics. This kind of migration by families bound by religion was common. A few minutes' drive away, a group of Shakers established a village at Pleasant Hill, which can be seen mostly unchanged today. The original Catholic settlement is gone, but there remains a large monastery at Gethsemane, a Catholic college (St. Catharine), and several small Catholic churches. Why the Maryland Catholics chose this area in particular is a matter of speculation, but for a number of reasons it later became the center of modern bourbon country, and many of these early Catholic settlers have become household names in bourbon.

In 1785, sixty families left St. Mary's County ("like the Israelites," declared the *Courier-Journal* in 1895), under the leadership of Basil Hayden, and settled on Pottinger's Creek in present-day Marion County. This group included Jeremiah Wathen, John Baptist Dant, Philip Mattingly, and many others whose names would have smaller roles in bourbon history. Pottinger's Station had been established by Samuel Pottinger, a Revolutionary War soldier who mustered in the area with Captain James Harrod and returned after the war in 1781. The Beam family, originally Böhm, first settled in Pennsylvania Dutch Country but moved south to Maryland and ended up traveling the Wilderness Road through the Cumberland Gap on or before 1778; Jacob first settled slightly upriver in a place called Crab Orchard and later built a farm distillery on Hardin's Creek in Manton. Thomas Lincoln (see page 58) was raising his son Abraham about ten miles away.

The settlers in this region worked together to raise families, go to church, grow crops, and distill whiskey. Joseph Washington Dant was particularly well regarded for his log-distilled whiskey, which he began making on his farm near Loretto in 1836. The log method of distillation involved hollowing out a wooden log, which was then split in half and clamped back in place with iron bands. Steam was run through a pipe or a coil inside the log and the distillate would have emerged from a cap into a worm. The second distillation would then pass through a much smaller copper still. For those who had run a small copper still for a while, this was a good way to increase production capacity with very little investment in new equipment. Later, the "log and copper" method of distilling would be improved with a three-chambered wood-stripping still, followed by a second distillation in a copper doubler. In 1870, Dant and his sons built a modern distillery at Dant's Station, not far from where the Maker's Mark distillery stands today, and situated such that nearly all of the process could be done by gravity. The mash tub was located highest in the factory; mash flowed from there into fermenters and down other pipes into the still. Unfilled case storage and bottling houses were

(Model.)

T. J. POTTINGER.
CONSTRUCTION OF WHISKY RACKS FOR BONDED WAREHOUSES.

No. 244,662. Patented July 19, 1881.

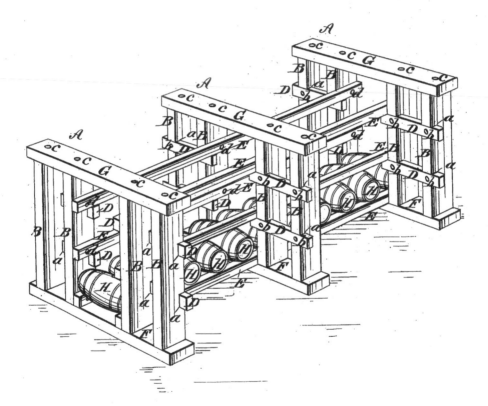

WITNESSES:

Donn J. Twitchell.

C. Sedgwick

INVENTOR:

T. J. Pottinger

BY Munn & Co

ATTORNEYS.

built lower down the hillside. A letter also exists showing four recipes for yeast that Dant used: for spontaneous, jug, day, and night yeast. Dant's whiskey became especially revered, and his Yellowstone brand of bourbon eventually became popular around the country. His sons and grandsons would start other distilleries: a large one in Gethsemane, and another distillery in Louisville to make Yellowstone.

The Pottinger family was equally as industrious. Samuel Pottinger's son founded a town just west of the initial settlement and named it New Haven after the town in Connecticut, which he thought to be the most beautiful he had ever seen while on a visit there. Pottinger's grandson, Thomas Jefferson, became a very successful distiller, and even filed for a patent on a warehousing technique in 1881. His distillery at Gethsemane would eventually be fully acquired by Minor Case Beam in 1900, making Old Trump and T. J. Pottinger brands.

Jacob Beam had three grandsons: Jim (we know), John (but who is always called Jack), and Joseph B. (not to be confused with his son Joseph L., who is also important). Jack was instrumental in starting the Early Times distillery, and his nephew by Joe B., Minor Case, may have learned to distill while working there. Early Times was a big operation, but Minor Case wanted to get out on his own, and he worked for seventeen years to acquire the old Pottinger distillery, then owned by Francis Head and Orene Parker. Minor Case's son, Guy, and Michael Dant, a son of J. W., married sisters, so they became partners, in a manner of speaking. The sisters must have been persuasive; hereafter the Beam family, which had been buried in the Protestant cemetery, would be buried across the road in the Catholic cemetery.

The end of Prohibition would mix things up a bit. After Prohibition, the sons and grandsons of Minor Case were increasingly removed from the distillery business, as fewer distilleries dotted the rural landscape and larger ones became giant factories. The Pottingers disappeared from the whiskey business. The Dants sold for around nine million dollars in 1944, a huge sum of money in those days. Minor Case's

---

T. J. Pottinger's patent for barrel warehousing

grandson Jimmy worked in distilleries here and there, but was often hired because he was a good baseball player and the inter-distillery baseball league needed his talent on the field. Jimmy would tell his son Steve that their side of the family was "blended, not bonded."

Steve Beam, who is very much an alive distiller, married a Dant, further cementing his family ties to history, and started a craft distillery, Limestone Branch, in Lebanon, Kentucky. Asked why so many families got into distilling, and how distilling became so entrenched in the family legacies, he suggested that it was just a reality of small-town life. These families were attending the same weddings and funerals, watching one another rise and fall in business. While we assume that distilling concentrated in Kentucky because of unique geologic conditions that are somehow perfect for whiskey, that is probably no more true than for furniture making in North Carolina or carpet-weaving in Georgia. There were abundant local resources of corn and soft water, as there was wood or cotton in other areas for other industries. But the social geography and familial topography were probably much more important to the establishment of the distilling culture among the Catholic migrants to Nelson, Marion, and Washington counties. Even today, the communities seem to have a forever quality that suggests distilling, Catholicism, weddings and funerals, hard work, and baseball games might go on here for a long time yet to come.

Perhaps the best story to illustrate this was an episode that occurred at Tom Craven's house in Marion County in 1904. A neighbor had hit a vein of salt water while excavating for zinc, and there were rumors of an old Pawnee gold mine on his land. One day, four buggies arrived with Craven's son and four men introduced as Joe and Minor Beam, a Mr. Samuels, and a Mr. Dant—all very recognizable as whiskey men. The group went up a creek with a lunch pail and some whiskey bottles and started prospecting. They returned every day over the course of that summer and built a seventy-five-foot mine shaft. But by the end of the summer, they never found any gold and gave up, and it turns out they had commenced the entire project on the word of a traveler who found a rock on the bar of a local tavern and swore it was gold ore. When the flimsy truth of the operation came out, they didn't mind. They'd had a good time that summer, and even if they didn't find gold, they found good friends in one another's company and probably more than a little bourbon.

J. W. Dant

The bottling staff at Brown-Forman Distillery

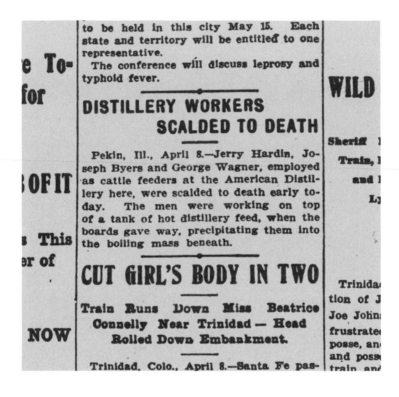

to be held in this city May 15. Each state and territory will be entitled to one representative.

The conference will discuss leprosy and typhoid fever.

DISTILLERY WORKERS SCALDED TO DEATH

Pekin, Ill., April 8.—Jerry Hardin, Joseph Byers and George Wagner, employed as cattle feeders at the American Distillery here, were scalded to death early today. The men were working on top of a tank of hot distillery feed, when the boards gave way, precipitating them into the boiling mass beneath.

CUT GIRL'S BODY IN TWO

Train Runs Down Miss Beatrice Connelly Near Trinidad — Head Rolled Down Embankment.

Trinidad, Colo., April 8.—Santa Fe pas-

WILD

Sheriff
Train,
and
L

Trinida
tion of J
Joe John
frustrate
posse, an
and poss
train an

Jerry Hardin, Joseph Byers,
and George Wagner
TOPEKA DAILY CAPITAL
APRIL 9, 1905

JASPER	"UNCLE"	LEMUEL
"JACK"	NEARIS	OSCAR
NEWTON	GREEN	MOTLOW
DANIEL		
	DISTILLER,	DISTILLER,
	FARMHAND,	BANKER,
DISTILLER	SLAVE	MULE TRADER
CA. 1850–1911	CA. 1820–1890	1869–1947
___	___	___
Lynchburg City Cemetery, Lynchburg, Tennessee	*Interment unknown*	*Lynchburg City Cemetery, Lynchburg, Tennessee*

Here's the part of the story you don't often hear: In 1909, Jack Daniel found religion and insisted that his name no longer be used to promote the whiskey that made him famous. Let's take a minute with that one.

Jack Daniel was born the tenth child of Calaway and Lucinda Daniel. His mother died shortly after he was born, possibly from complications from childbirth. Jack's father remarried quickly and had two more girls, and his stepmother doted on her blood-related children. The Civil War broke out when Daniel was around twelve, his father died when he was fifteen, and with his sisters married off and brothers moved away or fighting in the war and his stepmother looking to remarry, Jack was without a home.

He went to live with the Call family, whose Lutheran lay-minister patriarch, Dan, was fighting for the Confederacy with Nathan Bedford Forrest, and whose young wife, Mary Jane, could use a hand around the house and the family's general store. Call was still early in his career fathering eighteen children (yes), but even the three that were around were a lot for the twenty-year-old Mary Jane to manage.

Jack, who was short and boyish (he never grew taller than five foot two), was helpful enough, but as things settled after the war, he

Jack Daniel promoted his whiskey with the Silver Cornet Band

dreamed of a career beyond the farm, where his size would be less of a disadvantage. The Calls owned a few slaves before the war, and some stayed on even after earning their freedom. One, Nearis Green, served as the master distiller on the property. Uncle Nearis, as he was known, also played the fiddle and was a lively entertainer. Only a few years older than Jack, he taught him all about the still. Most farms of this size had stills, and the Call still, a mere eight gallons, was smaller than others in the county, but it did the job, making a gallon or two of whiskey in a run. Call and his wife also taught Jack to read and write. (Dan Call had himself been taken in as an orphan and saw Jack as a protégé of sorts.)

As Nearis ran the still, Jack went off to sell whiskey. When he turned twenty-five, he inherited a small amount of money from the sale of his family's farm, and he used it to go into business with a commercial distillery, in partnership with his old friend Dan Call. The new distillery used about a ton of grain (thirty-nine bushels) a day and could make almost one hundred gallons. After the Whiskey Ring scandal, in which distillers colluded to defraud the government of excise tax by recording less whiskey produced than there actually was, distillers were mandated to make three gallons for every bushel of grain they took in, so that output could be standardized based on grain consumed. This, in effect, legislated low-quality whiskey—good whiskey is made with narrower cuts that produce lower yields—but despite sending a coalition of Lynchburg distillers to Washington to argue their case, Daniel and his fellow whiskey makers had to conform to the new requirement.

The temperance movement eventually claimed Call, who had an increasingly difficult time squaring his ministerial work in the Lutheran Church with his distilling. By 1882, Daniel was on his own in the business. Soon, his No. 7 whiskey, named fondly after his first registered distillery number (distillers are all obsessive numerologists when it comes to their registered distillery numbers) came to be well known. Government reorganization of his revenue district forced Daniel to take a different number, so by putting "Old No. 7" on his label, he helped customers understand that the whiskey from No. 16 was the same stuff they used to like from No. 7. In 1884, he moved the distillery to its current site in Lynchburg to take advantage of the limestone spring that flowed from a scenic cave. In 1885, corn displaced rye as the more popular grain from which to make whiskey (a position it has held ever since), and Daniel's sour-mash, charcoal-mellowed whiskey stood out from cheaper whiskeys as customers got more particular about what they drank. Still, Daniel was as much a whiskey dealer as distiller. He bought whiskey stocks from other distilleries when prudent, which helped him expand sales when demand allowed.

Daniel hired a nephew, Lem Motlow, and taught him the business. He also hired Nearis's children and created contests around the distillery for the best still hand. One test was to lift a four-hundred-pound barrel on one knee and drink from the bunghole while holding it steady. Daniel "loved fine horses," according to grandnephew Felix Motlow. "He kept two thoroughbred Kentucky horses and drove one of those spirited horses from his home to his place of business." The still hands had a gag where they stood under one of Daniel's horses and lifted it for the amusement of visitors. Recognizing that amusement sometimes behooves the distiller, Daniel organized the Silver Cornet Brass Band in 1892 to play distillery functions, town parades, and funerals around Lynchburg.

Daniel never married, although he once asked a pianist thirty-five years his junior to be his wife. Her father declined and Jack attended her wedding some time later, giving her a ten-dollar gold piece.

Daniel's whiskey was now being sold in bottles, and the square shape was something he thought would make the whiskey distinctive (and would travel efficiently in boxes and crates). In 1904, his whiskey won a gold medal at the Louisiana Purchase Exposition in Saint Louis (as anyone who's read the bottle knows). And then, as it is told, one morning Daniel arrived at work before anyone else and, forgetting the combination to his safe, kicked it with his foot in frustration. His toe swelled up, the injury proved fierce and stubborn, and Daniel died from the wound.

At least that's the story, and it's true, mostly. He actually lived for a few years thereafter, walking with a cane for a while, then bedridden and trapped in his house, though it was probably his poor diet and stress that eventually did him in, in October 1911. With temperance forces swirling around Tennessee, it was easy to see that his life's work might be ended by the stroke of a pen in Nashville. He willed his distillery to nephews Lem Motlow and Dick Daniel in 1907. Lem bought Dick out for ten thousand dollars, knowing that his heart wasn't in the game.

Tennessee did go dry. Gubernatorial candidate Edward Ward Carmack, a fiercely dry Prohibitionist, squared off with incumbent Malcolm Patterson, who favored local-option laws. Carmack lost the primary but held a grudge. The two met on a Nashville street in 1908 and drew pistols. When the gunfire ended, Carmack was dead. Dry forces turned him into a hero, and this incident swiftly mobilized the state legislature to pass laws first prohibiting the sale of alcohol, followed a year later by prohibiting the manufacture of alcohol. Lem moved the whiskey barrels and some distilling equipment to Saint Louis in the hopes of saving the business.

Newspapers reported that Jack Daniel got saved in 1909 and no longer wanted his name on whiskey. The first part is accurate. Daniel had participated in church functions as a community member, but never as a believer, though when contemplating his legacy, he joined the church and distanced himself from his whiskey. With the distillery being dismantled and moved, he may also no longer have wanted anything to do with a business that appeared to be sinking in a sea of opposition, and which he could no longer personally oversee. Near his headstone, two cast-iron chairs were placed, to accommodate female mourners. The chairs remain.

Motlow picked up where Daniel gave in. He sold much of his Saint Louis distillery to George Remus (see page 155). He got staggeringly drunk on a train to Saint Louis and shot a conductor during an altercation with a black porter. He hired several high-powered lawyers to blame the altercation on the porter, and the all-white jury acquitted him. The justice department sued him for his business with Remus but later dropped the case. The old Lynchburg distillery burned. When Prohibition ended, Motlow petitioned the state to build a distillery to sell whiskey out of state, but the Lynchburg residents resisted. He worked around them and eventually got permission. His Jack Daniel's distillery reopened in 1938, and though he had a stroke a year later, Motlow wasn't going to let physical incapacity hold him back as it had done for his uncle. He went to work in a wheelchair. He also discouraged his four sons from marrying, thinking that women would distract them from the distillery business.

Motlow died in 1947; that same year, his sons sold the business to Brown-Forman.

Jack Daniel

The safe that killed him

A continuous copper column still at the O.F.C. distillery
in Frankfort, Kentucky, around 1890

An illegal continuous copper column
still in a warehouse in Chicago, 1931

	HENRY	
ABRAHAM	CLAY	ANDREW
OVERHOLT	FRICK	MELLON

	INDUSTRIALIST,	
	PHILANTHROPIST,	SECRETARY OF THE
DISTILLER	DISTILLERY	TREASURY,
	BOOKKEEPER	DISTILLERY OWNER
	AND OWNER	

| 1784–1870 | 1849–1919 | 1855–1937 |

Mount Pleasant	Homewood Cemetery,	Trinity Episcopal Church
Cemetery,	Pittsburgh,	Cemetery,
Mount Pleasant,	Pennsylvania	Upperville, Virginia
Pennsylvania		

Western Pennsylvania had always been fertile ground for distillers (see John Neville, page 39) and its rye whiskey often appreciated as emblematic of the spirit of the frontier, of rebellion, and of the rural mountaineer of the northern Appalachians. While historians have often focused on settlers of Scotch or Irish descent, there were also many Germans in the area, many of whom were more industrious at making whiskey. And while Pennsylvania long ceded its title as a whiskey-making state, its influence persists in ways that are written into the fabric of our economy. Take, for example, Henry Clay Frick.

Henry Oberholtzer, a Mennonite and distiller from Bucks County, moved west in 1800 with his wife and settled at Broad Ford, Pennsylvania, with his twelve children, including Abraham, whose surname would later be simplified to Overholt. Abraham, already sixteen at the time of the move, started contributing to the family farm by weaving, but after working the loom in his early years he became more interested in distilling. The whiskey from the Overholt farm on the Youghiogheny River earned a reputation, and traders could command higher prices for his barrels, prompting Abraham to expand the distillery business. In 1859, Overholt built a new distillery, six stories high and one hundred feet long, whose building still stands in West Overton. (The modern-era distillery, now defunct, stands on the river at Broad Ford.)

Overholt's rye-based whiskey came to represent the whiskey of the Monongahela region; it was reportedly favored by Doc Holliday (this is likely), Ulysses S. Grant (plausible), and Abraham Lincoln (specious). Abraham died in 1870, and though his son Henry Stauffer had inherited some of the day-to-day operation, it was one of his grandchildren, by his daughter Elizabeth, who would eventually run the company.

Henry Clay Frick, born in 1849, was never that interested in the distillery business. After working in a shop in Pittsburgh, an illness sent him back to the family farm, where he ended up clerking in the distillery office and rising quickly to a management position. But Frick was most interested in coal—and, by extension, coke, iron, and steel—and used his earnings from the distillery to buy the mineral rights to many coal seams in Western Pennsylvania. When he ran out of money, he went to Pittsburgh to approach Judge Thomas Mellon for a loan. Frick expected a friendly audience: The Mellons once lived in Westmoreland County, and Judge Thomas knew his mother when they were younger.

In fact, Judge Thomas's father had been a distiller, and the boy had assisted him in setting up a crude still to convert his family's peaches and apples to brandy when there was no immediate market for the produce. He wrote in his autobiography that two rock outcroppings in the ravine above their farm supported a straw roof with a cool spring running through the improvised structure, perfect for supporting a still. Young Thomas gathered peaches and apples, counting it as some of the hardest work he'd ever done, hauling them in bushels to the still house. So it was not a stretch that Frick found favor with the Mellons, became fast friends with Thomas's son Andrew, and with loans from the Mellon Bank, Frick acquired more mineral rights and was quickly controlling 80 percent of the coal output in Western Pennsylvania.

In 1879, Frick had achieved his life's ambition, to be a millionaire by the age of thirty. He celebrated with a Havana cigar. In the next two years, he outmaneuvered other relatives and came to control the family's distillery business, as well as the world-famous A. Overholt & Co. and Old Farm brands. He was ruthlessly obsessed with increasing his own wealth, at any cost. In an effort to boost his profits, he built houses near his mines and rented them to miners. He set up company stores and paid his employees in scrip, redeemable only at those stores. He hired Pinkerton strike-breakers to shut down labor organization. He built railroads and charged others to use them. He was shot twice in the neck during an assassination attempt by an anarchist and labor sympathizer.

And if these aspects of Frick's character seem ruthless, nothing quite matches the Johnstown Flood, wherein a dam collapsed at his private hunting club, which he shared with Mellon, Andrew Carnegie, and other industrialists. Due to poor maintenance, the dam's failure sent a wall of water downstream that killed 2,209 people and destroyed entire towns. Frick and his partners successfully avoided criminal prosecution or legal culpability, though Frick donated to recovery efforts.

By the 1880s, Frick was in an uneasy partnership with Carnegie and quickly becoming one of the richest people in the world. Still, he probably kept a soft place in his heart for the distillery. He made arrangements to lease it, then sued to get it back. He made deals with the Mellon family to share the ownership, and upon his death in 1919, a controlling stake passed to his long-time friend Andrew Mellon, probably the only person he trusted with it.

Shortly after, Mellon was nominated as secretary of the Treasury—a position once held by the foe of Western Pennsylvania distillers, Alexander Hamilton—and served from 1921 to 1932, placing him in the awkward position of owning a distillery during a time when distilling was banned. Still (and perhaps not coincidentally), the Old Overholt distillery was one of a few distilleries that were permitted to make medicinal whiskey, and it operated during the later parts of the Prohibition era.

It's possible Mellon never had the same fire for the alcohol business as his friend Clay. In 1900, when he was forty-five, he married the twenty-one-year-old daughter of one of the owners of the Guinness brewery, Nora Mary McMullen, but the two divorced acrimoniously in 1912. Mellon never remarried; their son would go on to breed racehorses. Years later, Mellon was impeached for financing an army of homeless Pennsylvanians who marched on Washington in protest, known as Cox's Army, a politically complicated act that seemed to contradict his place in Hoover's administration. His conduct was called into question, his ownership of the distillery during Prohibition scrutinized, and he resigned and retired to private life. Mellon sold the distillery to Seton Porter, whose National Distillers would consolidate many of the brands produced by regional distilleries like Overholt.

The Guinness company grew to become the largest liquor company in the world, now called Diageo, maker of Johnnie Walker, Bulleit Bourbon, and George Dickel. Henry Clay Frick's art collection can be seen at the Frick Collection, an idiosyncratic gallery housed in his former mansion in New York City's Upper East Side. Andrew Mellon's collection would become a significant part of the National Gallery of Art. And the Old Overholt brand of rye whiskey is still being made, though it is now distilled in Kentucky by Beam Suntory.

The Johnstown Flood

JOHN
DALY
FIREMAN

FRANK
TRENNOR
ASSISTANT FIREMAN

JOSEPH
AND
MRS. HORAKA
SHAVING-PUSHER

SANDY
MILLER

FRANK
PODRATZ
COAL-WHEELER

JACOB
KAKUSKA
ENGINEER

ALL DIED 1880

Interments generally unknown;

Kakuska is buried in Bohemian National Cemetery, Chicago, Illinois

U nder the massive headline "BLOWN TO ETERNITY," the *Chicago Tribune* described the explosion of a steam cooker at Simon Powell & Sons Distillery in 1880, which was located at South Canalport Avenue and South Morgan Street. The engineer had built a pressure cooker for the mash, which was desired to improve efficiency at the distillery, though at the time of the accident, it had been used only a few times. The distiller on duty had a clog in the line and directed the engineer to increase the steam to blow the clog through. The boiler exploded. "It was blown through the roof, and went almost straight up into the air, some say until it looked no larger than a flour-barrel. The main portion landed on the west side of Morgan Street, about 175 feet west and a little to the north of its original location . . . the jagged edge of the riven iron looked like a mammoth fruit can which had been chopped open with a dull instrument."

Six died in the explosion, including Sandy (his last name went unrecorded), a Scotsman who was mortally injured by the concussion and scalding, his body "badly mangled and so horribly scalded that the skin and portions of the flesh peeled off to the touch." When fireman Daly's wife found her husband's body, "her grief became uncontrollable, and it was with great difficulty that she was taken from the room to prevent her from throwing herself prostrate upon the disfigured remains."

The saddest story of all was Joseph Horaka, whose wife was bringing him supper at the time of the explosion. Both were buried in the wreckage. "In the mass of bricks and shavings a young man found a shawl and a piece of a dress. 'Here's the woman,' he shouted, and immediately a crowd gathered about him. A few began digging into the shaving with their hands, and soon a slipper and a dinner-pail were brought out." But after several hours of digging the bodies could not be found. Their fifteen-year-old daughter came to the scene, "crying as if her heart would break," whereupon she claimed the shawl and other articles. "She identified them all at once. But even this did not add to her already strong conviction that both her parents were in the ruins."

EXPLOSION IN A DISTILLERY.

FIVE MEN KILLED AND NINE SEVERELY OR FATALLY INJURED.

CINCINNATI, Oct. 20.—A dispatch from Terre Haute, Ind., to the *Commercial* says: " At 3 o'clock this afternoon the boilers in Cox & Fair. bank's distillery, one of the largest in the country, exploded and set the building on fire. The wildest excitement prevailed. The Fire Department, with the aid of the Police and citizens, soon subdued the flames, and then extricated the workmen who had. been buried in the débris caused by the explosion. Five men were instantly killed. They were: Joseph Denny, fireman; John Brooks, bricklayer; Harvey Day, (colored,) laborer; William Bergman, and M. K. Reilley. The last named was an employe of John V. Nicolai & Co., of Cincinnati, and was superintending work in the distillery.

The injured are Frank Stanley, fireman, both legs and arms broken, fatally injured; Henry Wilson, wounded about the head. in a critical condition; Eugene Mehring, head bruised, will probably recover; William Kirtley, 15 years old, arms broken and badly scalded, a fatal case; Henry Dinky, scalded and bruised; Frank Brown, arm broken; Washburn Simpson, John Young, and George Trout, skulls fractured. Charles ;G. Foote, the head engineer, had just left the distillery before the explosion occurred, and says the boilers were carrying 90 pounds of steam. One entire battery of three boilers exploded. The loss to the distillery is about $8,000.

Joseph Denny, John Brooks, Harvey Day,
William Bergman, and M. K. Reilley
THE *NEW YORK TIMES*,
OCTOBER 20, 1880

BLOWN TO PIECES.

EXPLOSION IN AN ILLINOIS DISTILLERY WITH FATAL RESULTS.

CHICAGO, Sept. 10.—The Enterprise Distillery at Pekin was totally wrecked at 7 o'clock this morning by the explosion of a patent cooker. This is a new invention in distilling, and is calculated to greatly increase the speed facilities of a mill. In this instance the cooker was an iron shell similar to an ordinary boiler. It is a scientific fact that in its ordinary use a latent heat is developed from the meal after the steam is turned off and the vacuum pump started. Unless closely guarded an explosion must result. In this instance the material used in the construction of the cooker was old and worn. The house occupied by the distillery people is owned by Edward Spellman, J. Doheny, and T. Killien, all of Peoria. The loss to the firm is fully $4,000.

Immediately after the explosion, which was imperfectly heard in Pekin, owing to the distance, a general alarm was sounded. Those first on the ground saw a terrible sight. The mammoth structure, covering 300 feet of ground, was spread over 10 acres of space. Lying against a tub on the river side were the mangled remains of Andy Duffin, Superintendent of the cookers. The lower part of his head was blown off and his body was terribly mutilated. The men in the ruins were still alive, and saws and axes were brought into play. Thomas Hieronymous, storekeeper, brother of a prominent banker, was found slightly scalded and almost overcome by the intense heat. The shrieks of Engineer Christian Hattey could be plainly heard. He was found pinioned by cross timbers, terribly scalded, and exposed to intense heat. He was rescued, but has died before this. Edward Welch, a young man about town; Alexander Duffin, yeast maker, and a brother of Andrew, and a strange man are still buried in the ruins. The father of the Duffin boys is reported insane.

Andy Duffin and Christian Hattey
THE NEW YORK TIMES,
SEPTEMBER 11, 1884

MARIA DISTASIO

VICTIM OF MOLASSES FLOOD

1908–1919

___

St. Michael Cemetery, Boston, Massachusetts

Maria Distasio, ten years old, was often sent out on her lunch break from Paul Revere Elementary on Prince Street to gather miscellaneous bits of wood or broken pallets to use as firewood from the loading docks of the busy commercial warehouse district next to her family's home in Boston's North End. Maria would often go to play with downstairs neighbors Pasquale and Vincenzo Iantosca. The trio would sometimes bring buckets to the base of the large molasses tank that leaked rivers of sticky liquid from its riveted steel plate enclosure, to the annoyance of the watchmen who guarded the tank from troublemakers.

The United States Industrial Alcohol Company operated a distilling plant in Cambridge, and molasses would be transported by ship from the Caribbean to Boston Harbor, where it would stay in a large holding tank that had been quickly constructed in advance of American entry into World War I, before being transported by elevated rail in smaller tanks to the distillery. The spirit produced was a neutral alcohol intended for industrial use in the production of munitions. By January 1919, the war was practically over, but the company was running full tilt, and some have speculated that the distillery was being run overtime in order to produce an inventory of rum before Prohibition.

Maria was in the middle of being lectured by two adults when the tank gave way. A tidal wave of 2.3 million gallons of molasses was probably twenty-five feet high and traveling thirty-five miles an hour when it hit her. A firefighter spotted Maria by a tangle of hair floating on the surface of the molasses. She had drowned, along with many others who had asphyxiated by drowning in molasses or were crushed by debris from buildings that had been reduced to sticks by the force of the flood.

Charles Cameron Burnap was a seventeen-year-old merchant marine, working aboard the *Nantucket,* which was docked near the molasses tank. He and his fellow crew members rushed to assist the victims in the aftermath of the flood, and he wrote the following in a letter to his mother:

> There was no explosion; only a loud hissing as the tank burst and the two million gallons of molasses came flooding out. It swept houses and everything out into the middle of the park where we drill and piled them up in great wrecks. The molasses was from two to four feet deep and we had to wade around in this with all our clothes on, shoes leggings, jackets and sweaters for it was cold and we had time to take nothing off.
>
> Lots of people were drowned in the street by being knocked down with the force of the first flood of molasses. Once down under three feet of molasses it was impossible to get up without help because the molasses was so thick and it acted just like quicksand. The fellows from the *Nantucket* were the first on the scene and went right to work clearing the houses of people who were caught in them when the flood came. Most of them were caught and pinned way at the bottom of the wreckage and we had to use axes and crowbars to get at them, and some of the sights we had to look at were enough to turn a fellow's stomach, men and women with legs and arms gone insides squashed out. Eyes, ears, and jaws missing. They were all covered in molasses and so were we and it was hard to get any kind of hold on them to carry them away. Another fellow and I saw a pair of legs sticking up out of the molasses and we went to pull out what we thought was a person but nothing but two legs and a part of some hips came out when we pulled.
>
> We worked over an hour getting one man out who was caught under a building but was up out of the molasses

Boston Molasses Flood

so that he was not smothered. There was a door and two or three beams over him and his legs were caught in a pair of stairs. He certainly was game because he was talking to us most of the time and telling us what to do. The doctor gave him two shots of dope and a lot of whiskey.

USIA blamed the tank's failure on sabotage by anarchists, which was never proven nor seriously suspected. Maria Distasio's family was compensated three thousand dollars for their loss.

FROM THE *WEEKLY WISCONSIN*, JULY 1, 1885

LOUIS SCHERTZ

HIDDEN TREASURE. CINCINNATI, O., JUNE 20— *A story is published here of the finding of $75,000 in gold and silver coin, hidden in the walls and ceilings of a four-story building, 133 Court Street, by Louis Schertz, who occupied the place for years in the liquor business. He died recently and left to his brother a memorandum showing in what places money would be found, but did not indicate the amount. As the deceased had always appeared to be a poor man and lodged in the store-room, the finding of this large sum was a surprise. It is said he left valuable secrets in whisky compounding, rectifying and plans for the construction of distilleries.*

A TOUR OF CAVE HILL CEMETERY

CAVE HILL CEMETERY in Louisville is the final resting place of many distillers. The Cemetery is a classical example of the rural cemetery model and is still Louisville's premier cemetery. Founded in 1848, the cemetery is noted for its high concentration of military figures, whiskey distillers, and a particular fried-chicken personality.

1. GEORGE GARVIN BROWN
Founder of Brown-Forman (today makes Jack Daniels and Woodford Reserve), first distiller to sell exclusively by the bottle

2. MERIWETHER LEWIS CLARK
Grandson of William Clark, the explorer, and founder of Churchill Downs and the Kentucky Derby

3. WILLIAM LARUE WELLER
Louisville distiller and rectifier mostly selling wholesale whiskey

4. PAUL JONES
Founder of Four Roses, avid horseman

5. JULIAN VAN WINKLE
"Pappy" Van Winkle, distilled Old Fitzgerald and other whiskies at Stitzel-Weller; his son is buried here, too

6. COLONEL HARLAND SANDERS
Fried-chicken magnate, the "Jim Morrison" of Kentucky

7. T. JEREMIAH BEAM
Master distiller of Jim Beam immediately after Jim himself and before Booker Noe

8. ARTHUR PHILIP STITZEL
Son of Philip Stitzel, helped develop recipes at Stitzel-Weller with Elmo Beam, warehoused whiskey during Prohibition

9. FREDERICK STITZEL
Distillery builder, helped patent barrel rickhouses used throughout the industry

10. CAVE SPRING
This short limestone cave is where Cave Hill Cemetery derives its name, not open for spelunking

11. J. T. S. BROWN
Whiskey wholesaler and half-brother of George Garvin Brown

An eight-story aging warehouse at an unknown distillery

PAUL JONES

WHISKEY BROKER

1841–1895

Cave Hill Cemetery, Louisville, Kentucky

P aul Jones at least carries this distinction: He has the largest tomb of any of the distillers buried in Kentucky. He died a millionaire, which was no small feat in 1895, and his wealth came from whiskey. He created many brands, the most enduring of which is Four Roses.

Born in Lynchburg, Virginia, he fled with his family during the Civil War to Georgia. He and his brother Warner joined the Confederate Army, though Paul's "delicate health" prevented him from seeing much action. His brother died at the Battle of Atlanta.

After the war, Jones and his father sold whiskey and tobacco in Atlanta, and when the Georgia state legislature started yielding to temperance advocates, Jones moved north to Louisville, setting up in a wood-paneled office with mosaic tile floor. His business acumen was chiefly in marketing. His savvy was summarized in his obituary in the Louisville *Courier-Journal* by mention of his electric advertisement in Madison Square in New York that cost twelve hundred dollars a month.

Jones died a bachelor, which proves somewhat problematic for his lasting legacy, as the brand he founded is lately built on the myth that he married his sweetheart after she wore a corsage of four roses, signaling her acceptance of his proposal. Historian Mike Veach has speculated that the famous whiskey may simply have been a blend of four whiskeys from the R. M. Rose Company of Atlanta, Georgia, which sold several varieties of corn and rye whiskey using "Old-Fashioned Copper" stills. In fact, the first time the brand name appears is in an 1889 advertisement in the *Atlanta Journal-Constitution*. And the corsage story was once told in reverse: Jones's beloved spurned him, so he devoted his life to whiskey. The Four Roses distillery that is today in Lawrenceburg, Kentucky, was built fifteen years after Jones's death, and Jones was more a whiskey wholesaler and marketer than he was a distiller.

Jones had a penchant for fast horses, and, according to the *Courier-Journal*, "refused to let anyone pass him on the road." At the time of his death, he owned five fast trotters, though none should be confused with the horse Paul Jones that won the Kentucky Derby in 1920.

A whiskey broker's office in 1904. George Gavin Brown is far right

COLONEL EDMUND HAYNES TAYLOR JR.

DISTILLER, ENTREPRENEUR, AND LOBBYIST

1830–1923

Frankfort Cemetery, Franklin County, Kentucky

N o whiskey historian can resist hypothesizing, with total disregard for the futility of the enterprise, on the inventor of bourbon. Never mind that bourbon always was—that there is no evidence that whiskey was ever *not* made from corn in the United States or ever *not* aged in charred barrels. Aged whiskey appears in advertisements around 1800, and ten-year-old whiskey was already being advertised in New Orleans in 1840.

Nonetheless, there have been many names thrown into the ring: Elijah Craig and Evan Williams are often nominated, and they are aided significantly by the marketing campaigns from the companies that make the whiskeys that now bear their names. Old George Thorpe gets a nod in at least two historical books, as do a number of candidates (Jacob Myers, Joseph and Samuel Davis, John Corliss, and the Tarascon brothers) courtesy of Mike Veach's excellent bourbon history.

But if we are to credit these men as the founding fathers of bourbon, it was E. H. Taylor Jr. who saved bourbon from itself; consider him the spirit's Abraham Lincoln.

Taylor was born well-off in Columbia, Kentucky. His father, a merchant trader who frequently traveled to New Orleans, died of typhus when Taylor was young, and for a time he lived with his great-uncle Zachary Taylor, who would serve as our twelfth president until his death in office. Uncle Zachary was a career general, and a lingering aphorism from his battle days—"General Taylor Never Surrenders"—followed in the family line.

Taylor spent his early years in banking and commodities trading, but with much of the South reeling from the war, Taylor entered into an industry that he imagined would bounce back quickly: the whiskey business. He set up an office in 1864, and in 1866 he traveled to Europe to explore the latest in distillery technologies. In 1869, he purchased the Swigert distillery and renamed it the O.F.C. distillery, which by most accounts stood for Old-Fashioned Copper (though George Stagg, the next owner, would later alter this to Old Fire Copper). The distillery used old-fashioned techniques (copious copper, low-distillation proof, limestone water) and new technologies like column stills to make whiskey. His brick warehouses were steam-heated in cycles, ensuring that the bourbon developed a rich and full flavor through a controlled aging process.

Taylor was as much a promoter as a distiller. Since his customers (retail stores or saloons) purchased whiskey by the barrel, he insisted they be cleaned up and fitted with brass rings. He offered letters of recommendation and prints of his distillery to wholesalers and retailers visiting the O.F.C. distillery, an early effort at marketing his products.

More important, Taylor became involved in protecting bourbon whiskey's name from imitators. In those days (as now), many distillers would buy a commercially distilled whiskey in bulk, and bottle or package that whiskey under their own name. In most cases back then, this bulk whiskey was rectified whiskey, an inexpensive neutral spirit to which wood chips, glycerin, caramel coloring, and other adulterants were added to mimic the taste of bourbon. A generation before Taylor, "Old Whiskey" was shorthand for the best; Taylor helped make "Pure Whiskey" a whiskey advertiser's most meaningful claim.

Taylor came to distilling from the finance and marketing aspect of the business, and thus was familiar with the mechanisms of power around business. He filed at least fourteen lawsuits to protect his trademark, according to Kentucky legal scholar Brian Haara. Taylor was also mayor of Frankfort, Kentucky, for most of the 1870s and 1880s. With the help of then U.S. Treasury Secretary John G. Carlisle (also from Kentucky), Taylor drafted the architecture for a federal guarantee of whiskey provenance, though courts were quick to insist that this was not the same as quality.

The Bottled-in-Bond Act of 1897 stipulates the highest class of American whiskey, more rigorous than any whiskey laws in any country before or since. To bear the "bottled in bond" designation, a whiskey must otherwise meet the criteria for straight whiskey, be distilled by a single distiller at one distillery in a single distilling season, be at least four years old, and be bottled at one hundred proof. The law has changed somewhat, mostly at the level of government supervision and the tax stamp requirements, but the thrust is the same: With a bonded bottle, you know where it comes from. It's something that today's consumers could use a little more often.

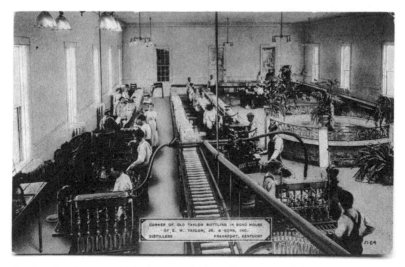

The bottling line at Old Taylor was designed as a part of the tour to reinforce the integrity of whiskey bottled at the distillery

The Old Taylor Distillery attracted the general public as a tourist attraction

At some point, Taylor began a private correspondence with Harvey Washington Wiley (see page 144), and sent his son to testify on behalf of straight whiskey producers in hearings on the Pure Food and Drug Act of 1906, supporting truth-in-labeling requirements as part of a broader public concern over adulterated foods and the conditions of industrial production, given some recent public visibility through Upton Sinclair's influential book *The Jungle*.

Taylor also invented one other thing of note: the distillery tour. Taylor felt that transparency was his great advantage in the marketplace. And so, in 1887, on Glenn's Creek just south of Frankfort, he built a castle to whiskey. It was a more modern and elaborate version of the O.F.C. distillery he had purchased a few years before. And by inviting the public to visit, Taylor could connect directly to his eventual customers, not just the stores and saloons buying wholesale by the barrel. Trains would stop nearby so that passengers could enjoy the distillery's grounds, with its main building of stone and crenelated battlements, a Roman fountain room where pools of limestone water reminded customers of the virtues of Kentucky's geography, and a sunken rose garden planted perhaps in an effort to appeal to those that might not be as excited about a distillery tour (wives). Visitors left with a complimentary "tenth pint" bottle, which is likely the best tour souvenir ever offered, then or since.

A fire broke out at the James E. Pepper distillery in Lexington in 1934

A HORRIBLE DEATH.

Mr. H. E. Pogue, the Distiller, Caught in the Machinery at His Establishment

And His Life is Crushed Out—Particulars of the Terrible Accident.

Mr. Henry E. Pogue met with a horrible death about ten o'clock this morning.

He was caught in some of the machinery at the Pogue & Thomas distillery in the West End, and the next instant his life was crushed out.

Mr. Patrick Fox, who is employed about the establishment, saw him only a few minutes before the accident happened.

Mr. Fox was branding barrels in a car on the side track back of the buildings at the time. Some parties were standing about, when Mr. Pogue came along and requested them to keep out of Mr. Fox's way. He then went on into the building.

"It was only about three minutes afterwards," said Mr. Fox, "when Mr. Pogue's son Henry came running to me and said his father was dead."

No one witnessed the awful accident. It seems that Mr. Pogue, after leaving Mr. Fox, went into the building and up on the second floor. Here it is supposed he started to oil some of the machinery, or fix it.

While thus engaged his clothing was caught in a cog-wheel and an upright shaft, and the unfortunate man, caught in the relentless grasp of the machinery, was drawn in and wound about the shaft.

His body was crushed and mangled in a horrible manner. Nearly every bone from his chest down was broken and crushed, and one leg was almost torn from the body.

Henry E. Pogue
THE MAYSVILLE *EVENING BULLETIN*,
NOVEMBER 14, 1890

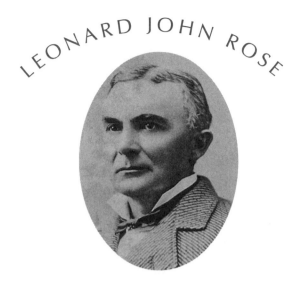

LEONARD JOHN ROSE

VINTNER, HORSE RACER, AND DISTILLER

1827–1899

Evergreen Cemetery, Los Angeles, California

Despite its overwhelming contribution to the nation's agricultural output, the West Coast has never had its fair share of distilleries. This may be because wine and beer were easily and excellently made, so there was not often reason to distill those products into other commodities. Also, the West was settled mostly after the advent of rail travel, and the early economic incentives for distillation, such as the reduction in weight of a commercial crop, no longer mattered as much.

Still, there is a history, if mostly forgotten. Consider Leonard John Rose, who was born in Bavaria and immigrated to New Orleans as a boy. He moved his family westward, surviving an Indian attack near the Colorado River in Arizona and finally settled in Los Angeles in 1860. He grew lemon, orange, and olive trees, but he was best known for his vineyards, with grapes imported from Spain, Italy, and Peru. The farmhouse, known as Sunny Slope, a pre–Civil War structure, still stands in San Gabriel. The Lamanda Park neighborhood in Pasadena is a portmanteau of his first initial and his wife's first name. He was also an avid breeder of fast horses and his breeding ranch Rosemead would one day become the city of the same name.

An 1886 article in the *Los Angeles Herald* paints Rose as a savior of the wine growers of Southern California. Grapes were looking to command such a low price that year that harvesting them wouldn't even be worth it. Rose advocated for building a distillery, and a building on the other side of the Los Angeles River (accessible then via a covered bridge) was refurbished so as to produce a commodity from the grapes that could withstand fluctuations in price over the seasons.

The idea proved popular, and shares of the start-up distillery quickly went up in value. Zinfandel, muscat, and mission grapes poured into the distillery by the wagonload. As many as thirty-five four-horse teams were waiting with carts of grapes to be discharged. A fifteen-foot-diameter crusher, run with steam power, crushed the grapes into juice and pomace. The mixture was then conveyed to one of thirty-two seven-thousand-gallon vats, where it would ferment for eight days. A sluice conveyed the liquid to a ten-thousand-gallon concrete tank and then into a twenty-six-foot-tall wooden stripping still. The low-proof liquid that emerged was called singlings. Some of it was sent back to the pomace tank to feed into the strip still, but higher-poof liquor was sent to a copper-pot still for a secondary, polishing distillation. The emerging distillate—a clear, high-proof brandy—was diluted, barreled, and readied for sale. On a single day, there was enough pomace to produce seventeen thousand gallons of brandy.

Despite Rose's success as a businessman, trade organizer, and politician, by 1899, his finances were in ruin. One day, after failing to secure a loan in San Francisco and later in Ventura, Rose told his wife that he would travel upstate on business. Instead, he secretly spent the evening at the family mansion, on Grand Avenue and Fourth Street in the Bunker Hill area of Los Angeles. He wrote his family a farewell note, stating that his financial difficulties were too much to bear. Also included was a postscript: "You will find my remains in the chicken yard."

The note was received the following morning. No one at the house really wanted to run out and look at the backyard, so Rose's son-in-law was called from his office downtown to inspect. He found, the *Los Angeles Times* wrote, "his father-in-law lying face downward in a little hollow at the rear of the lot. His head reclined on his hat, and in one hand was clasped a bunch of carnations." To everyone's surprise, Rose was not dead—not yet, at least—and doctors were immediately summoned to revive him. But Rose had taken a lethal dose of morphine, and it eventually kicked in.

The family sold the mansion on Bunker Hill, and by 1937 it was in such disrepair that the house was dismantled. The following year, its wood paneling was salvaged and used in the 20th Century Fox feature *In Old Chicago*.

THE LOUISVILLE *COURIER-JOURNAL*,

SEPTEMBER 23, 1899

HANS HANSON

Hans Hanson, a resident of Cincinnati and a traveling salesman for a Louisville distillery, committed suicide at Monitowoc, Wisconsin, by shooting. On a card he had written: "Cause, madness and fear of lunatic asylum."

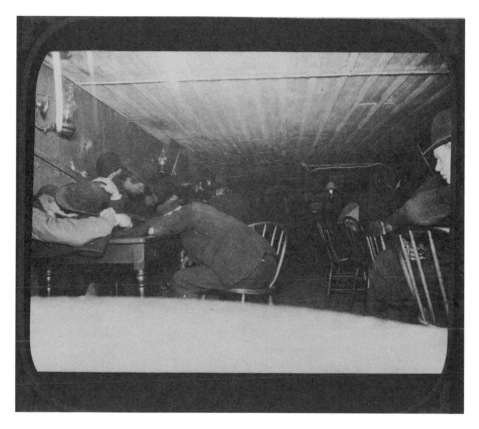

Drunks in a two-cent restaurant at
Mulberry Bend in Manhattan, ca. 1890

ISAAC WOLFE BERNHEIM

DISTILLER, NATURALIST, HORSE OWNER

1848–1945

Originally interred at Cave Hill Cemetery,
moved to Bernheim Forest, Clermont, Kentucky, in 1956

Isaac Wolfe Bernheim traveled as a young man to New York City from a small town near Freiburg, Germany, where he was born, hoping to take a job as a bookkeeper in a yarn-making factory for an uncle on Spring Street in Manhattan, but the firm was in trouble and the job evaporated as soon as Bernheim arrived off the boat, nineteen years old with twenty-five francs in his pocket. Cotton prices had fallen in 1867 and the country was still reeling from war. With no job, Bernheim made his way west as a peddler, working through Pennsylvania, and spending the winter in the town of Overton, where he danced at several square dances and attended quilting parties.

Bernheim eventually headed to Paducah, Kentucky, where his uncle had moved to open a general store, but he soon found better work as an accountant for a whiskey wholesaler. He rose quickly and became a salesman, bringing his younger brother Bernard over to work his former job. The two launched Bernheim Brothers and entered the liquor business.

They needed a brand, and so they invented I. W. Harper, using Isaac's first two initials and an all-American-sounding surname (it may have come from a celebrated horse trainer of the time, John Harper). They moved to Louisville, and in 1897, when a distillery they owned a stake in burned, they built a new one on what is today Bernheim Lane. The brothers eventually sold the business, and it bounced through a few hands. I. W. Harper was for a short time produced at Stitzel-Weller and became something of a cult product; it was discontinued in the United States until very recently. The Bernheim distillery moved to a new location, and a very modern iteration now makes whiskeys for Heaven Hill.

In 1922, Bernheim's wife died, and with the whiskey business defunct, Bernheim married her sister Emma and moved west, first to Denver, and later to California. At age ninety-six, despondent over an eye injury, Bernheim jumped to his death from the eighth floor of his oceanfront apartment in Santa Monica.

Bernheim gave fourteen thousand acres of land to the state of Kentucky as the Bernheim Forest, an arboretum about half an hour south of Louisville, where he is buried.

The Bernheim Brothers distillery in Louisville

A talent show put on by the foremen at Bernheim Brothers distillery

THE MAYSVILLE *EVENING BULLETIN*,

OCTOBER, 24, 1895

PETER AND HARRY GUBBARD

ILLICIT STILL CAUSES THE MURDER OF PETER AND HARRY GUBBARD IN JACKSON COUNTY, KY. LOUISVILLE, OCT. 24—*A double murder is reported from Jackson county, near the Mason county line. Peter and Henry Gubbard were shot and killed by Sanford Lakes, and the latter is now at large. The cause of the killing appears to be that about two years ago the Gubbard boys were instrumental in the discovery and destruction by revenue officials of an illicit still, operated by Lakes.*

WILLIAM JOHNSTON

MOONSHINER INFORMANT

DIED 1894

Interment unknown

One of the great legends of illegal whiskey surrounds the mostly true story of Lou Parris and Ralph Redmond, described in newspaper accounts as a "moonshine love story." Redmond belonged to a group of rural moonshiners in the hilly refuges of the Carolina Piedmont. Parris, the only daughter of a prominent family by one account, or eldest child of a poor widow in another, was, in either case, quite stunning. According to the *Washington Post*:

> The girl was as beautiful as a dewdrop and was the belle of the town. Her only deficiency was the lack of education. Her physical attainments were without a blemish. Her hair was the counterpart of the raven, and her eyes were so black that they scintillated like sparks in a night of impenetrable darkness. Her complexion was as white as the first gleam of sunrise. She was as modest and as pure as the blossom and bud and flowers on the shrubs and tress, whose company she kept every day of the spring-time.

Twenty-one-year-old Redmond knew a catch when he saw one. He courted Parris and the two fell in love, only to have the marriage forbidden by her family, who discovered Redmond's occupation.

Forbidden love being what it is, Parris had a hard time letting go. In time, a replacement arrived, in the form of the well-known and socially respected William Johnston (or Johnson in other accounts). Parris seemed to welcome Johnston's affection, but instead surreptitiously used Johnston's courtship as a cover for secret meetings with Redmond.

Eventually, Johnston found out what Parris was up to, but he kept quiet. Instead of confronting Parris, he focused his energies on his rival, and, as the *Saint Paul Globe* recounts, "did what to moonshiners is the meanest thing of which the human heart is capable. He led the 'revenues' to the illicit still." Redmond was arrested and jailed in Tyron City, though several Redmond family members "came down the mountain, battered in the doors of the prison and carried off their leader in triumph."

While Redmond was on the lam, Parris sent Johnston a note asking to meet. Once together, Parris murdered him in cold blood, plunging a penknife into his heart. She pled guilty to second-degree murder and served most of her sentence in a penitentiary. For good behavior, she was transferred to a Christian halfway house in Baltimore and secured a conditional pardon by Governor Elias Carr.

After Parris's release from the halfway house, she and Redmond were married in 1902 and relocated to Baltimore, where Redmond found work with a streetcar company.

Prohibition agents raid a moonshine still in Kentucky, 1931

FIRST PRESIDENT OF THE WHISKEY TRUST

1843–1918

————

Salem Fields Cemetery, Brooklyn, New York

Born in Austria, Joseph Benedict Greenhut moved to the United States as a boy and spent time in Mobile, Alabama, apprenticing to a tin- and coppersmith. He volunteered for the Union Army in 1861, reportedly the second man to enlist in the entire state. He was wounded at Fort Donelson but made his way back to the front line, serving at Gettysburg, Fredericksburg, and Chattanooga. He was a valiant soldier, and this legacy gave Greenhut many advantages in business over the course of his life.

Greenhut was a business person who capitalized on hype: His ventures were almost always fantastically successful, and then cataclysmic failures. Nearly every business that he started ended in some sort of dramatic implosion, and sketchy stories always swirled around them.

Greenhut moved to Peoria, Illinois, in 1866 and used his training as a coppersmith to start the Great Western distillery. This was a time when the distilling industry was starting to move out of the eastern strongholds like Brooklyn and Boston, and giant consolidated businesses were established to make neutral alcohol on giant column stills (also called cologne spirits). Compared with the existing distilleries south and east of the Ohio, these new ones mostly made bulk alcohol, much of it for industrial applications such as flame accelerants, perfumes, furniture polish, varnish, cooking fuel, and patent medicines. Some of this alcohol did become drinkable—it was blended with straight whiskey or other adulterants to make a cheap, light whiskey that could be sold to rectifiers, who would manipulate it further. This inexpensive whiskey was the spirit that made its way into the Great Plains for sale in the saloons and taverns of the Wild West.

In the late 1870s, demand surged abroad, as poor crops in Europe created a condition where American distilleries were exporting up to 20 percent of their output. When the European distilleries bounced back, American producers faced a glut, with inventory four times what the market demanded. Distilleries couldn't shut down, however, as they often existed in a symbiotic relationship with cattle lots (they needed to keep operating or they would lose the cattle business as well). For most of the 1880s, distillers struggled with wild swings in prices for their product.

In 1887, the Distillers' and Cattle Feeders' Trust, commonly known as the Whiskey Trust, was organized, with Greenhut as president. To join, a distiller had to reorganize as a corporation and offer its stock to nine trustees; he then expected to earn dividends according to the wisdom of the managers of the trust. The trust set prices for whiskey, dictated when distilleries could operate and at what capacity, and supervised recordkeeping.

Prominent holdouts included many of the Kentucky producers who were making straight whiskey, a different product that could be branded and marketed so as to command a premium over commodity prices. The Shufeldt distillery in Illinois also refused to participate, though it was near enough in geography to be ripe for intimidation. In 1888, sticks of dynamite were thrown on the roof of the distillery. In 1891, George Gibson, the trust's secretary, got caught in a sting operation trying to pay twenty-five thousand dollars to an undercover agent to bomb a Chicago distillery.

The trust was successful for a time, making as much as 90 to 95 percent of the alcohol consumed in the United States. It was also investigated by Congress for violating antitrust laws, and by 1895 it was bankrupt. The trust reorganized and disbanded several times in the years that followed, but public tastes had changed, and demand was rising for straight whiskeys made below the Ohio. (The Whiskey Trust distilleries continued through Prohibition and were reorganized by Seton Porter to become National Distillers Products Corporation, which, along with Schenley and Seagram, became one of the big three distillers of the post-Prohibition era.)

Greenhut also founded the Glucose Company of America. "The rapid advance of chemical science has opened a wide doorway for compounding mixtures so nearly resembling nature's products that the senses are impotent to the difference," wrote a House report of the 46th Congress, trying to articulate the public's wariness of industrial foods. Glucose was made from corn steeped first in hot water, then with sulfuric acid. Marble dust was added to neutralize the acid, and the resulting lime sulfate was filtered out. Glucose was far cheaper than cane sugar and was used in a variety of products: jellies, canned fruit and meat, syrups, and in honey jars with a little honeycomb. Food-labeling laws weren't what they are today, and the glucose sparked something of a public health crisis, as this artificial sugar from corn became viewed by the public as a health danger. (Sound familiar?) The company eventually dissolved—not for health concerns, but because it, too, was acting in violation of the Antitrust Act.

Greenhut's failures didn't stop him from investing in other businesses. He had interests in banks, cooperages, railways, and other companies. He moved to New York City, opening first the Siegel-Cooper dry goods store and, later, when mail-order business dried up and the business went bankrupt, a department store called the J. B. Greenhut Company. That store did well until the shopping district moved uptown, at which point it, too, went bankrupt. The building, on Eighteenth Street and Sixth Avenue, now houses a Bed Bath & Beyond.

Greenhut remains a major figure in Peoria history, having contributed to many civic improvements there, including the Grand Army of the Republic building and the Civil War Soldiers and Sailors Monument. His thirty-five-room mansion, once a spectacular vision of excess, still stands but has been carved up into apartments. His country home in New Jersey, Shadow Lawn, had been loaned to President Woodrow Wilson and became the "Summer White House;" it burned soon after Greenhut's death, in 1918.

JOKICHI TAKAMINE

WHISKEY SCIENTIST, ADRENALINE ISOLATOR,

CHERRY TREE PLANTER

1854–1922

Woodlawn Cemetery, Bronx, New York

Whiskey is an unfortunate footnote in Jokichi Takamine's career, though an important one that represents the intersection of science and distilling. Dr. Takamine's major contribution to whiskey-making was his understanding of diastase, an enzyme that breaks down starch into sugar, a fundamental requirement for making anything fermented or distilled from grain.

Takamine was born in Takaoka on the northwest coast of Japan. His father was a doctor; his mother came from a family of sake brewers. Sake is a fermented beverage made from steamed rice and a mold called aspergillus oryzae, which is used to begin fermentation. Koji, which describes both the mold and its fermented form, is used to make miso, soy sauce, and other traditional Japanese foods. In sake brewing, the koji is left to ferment for five to seven days. The mixture creates the necessary enzymes to catalyze the starch in the rice to sugars that can be fermented. Later, yeast is added to the mixture to convert the sugar to alcohol in different stages, yielding a much higher alcohol liquid.

Takamine studied this process in Osaka and Tokyo and did postgraduate work at the University of Glasgow in Scotland. He returned to Japan and worked for the government in agricultural research and development, but then, in 1884, when he attended the World's Fair and Cotton Centennial Exposition in New Orleans, he met an eighteen-year-old American woman, Caroline Hitch, and made plans to marry her.

Wanting to solidify his career before the nuptials, Takamine founded the Tokyo Artificial Fertilizer Company, which started importing large amounts of phosphate rock from South Carolina. In 1887, the couple visited several fertilizer companies on their honeymoon in Charleston, but they moved to Japan, where their sons were born.

Takamine later received a telegram from his mother-in-law, who had been advocating for his scientific discoveries in the States. She wrote that the whiskey industry in Chicago was particularly interested in his diastase enzyme. Joseph B. Greenhut (see page 137) first became interested in Takamine's processes and their applications for whiskey production.

Takamine had researched traditional Japanese industries, including sake brewing, for the Ministry of Agriculture and had speculated that koji could be used instead of malt to make whiskey. Beer and whiskey are both traditionally brewed by using the enzymes present in malted grain to convert starch to sugar, but Takamine's work isolating diastase (now called amylase) from koji could make the fermentation process more efficient, and obviated the need for malt in a whiskey mash bill, removing a costly step from the whiskey-making process.

Greenhut was president of the Whiskey Trust at the time and thought this would improve operations for its member companies. In 1891, the two announced a partnership. Bolstered by this deal, Greenhut built the largest distillery in the country, the Manhattan Distillery, in Peoria. Takamine moved to Peoria and set up a laboratory he called the White House. The *Chicago Daily Tribune* was quite taken with Dr. Takamine and erroneously suggested that "a species of bugs found on the rice is used instead of yeast." Takamine eventually used wheat bran as a base for his koji.

The maltsters, of course, protested this new technology. In October 1891, a mysterious fire burned one of the buildings in the distillery, just days after Takamine's new machinery had been installed. Greenhut hoped to rebuild the equipment and continue the experiment, but political pressure forced the trust into receivership just around the same time Takamine developed a serious liver condition. It took him months to recover, but his first order of business was to sue the trust. Takamine had put years into his whiskey improvements, but in the end they were never implemented on any scale at any distillery.

Still, his work in enzymes had substantial scientific value, and the pharmaceutical company Parke, Davis and Company had begun marketing his diastase as a digestive drug, with great success. By 1897, Takamine was in a position to move to New York to focus exclusively on medical research, being interested in the work of John Jacob Abel, a chemist who had just isolated epinephrine. At the urging of Parke, Davis and Company, Takamine worked on isolating adrenaline in sheep, and a young lab assistant, Keizo Uenaka, was the first to do so. It was the first hormone to be isolated in pure form.

Twelve years later, after reaping the financial rewards from his work in enzymes and hormones, Takamine had become a very prominent and wealthy man and wanted to give something back to his adopted country. He financed the planting of cherry blossom trees around the tidal basin in Washington, D.C., as a gesture of friendship between the United States and Japan. In all, 3,020 cherry trees were imported and planted over the next decade, where they can be seen today, in positions of prominence on the National Mall.

TERRIBLE EXPLOSION IN DISTLLING PLANT

Six Persons Killed and Many Injured.

A LIST OF THE CASUALTIES.

At Peoria, Ills., In the Corning Distilling Company's Plant Disastrous Explosion Occurs Dealing Out Death and Wrecking the Plant.

Peoria, Ill., Oct. 3.—One of the immense cookers in the main building of the Corning Distilling company's plant exploded this morning, killing several of the employes, maiming many more and wrecking that portion of the distillery.

The wreckage did not take fire and the firemen who had been summoned assisted the distillery employes, who had escaped, in the rescue of their less fortunate workmen.

Th cooker is a steel contrivance 20 feet in diameter and 80 feet in length and is used in cooking the mashes. It is presumed a vacuum was formed and when the steam was turned on to cook today's mash the explosion followed. The cooker was hurled through the north wall of the 4-story structure, a distance of 250 feet.

The entire north wall of the distillery was blown down, the south and east walls were badly damaged and wreckage was scattered all over the neighborhood. The distillery management esimate their loss at fully $75,000.

James McManues, Neil Powell, James O'Keefe, George Schaffer, John Wilson, and Guy Brennan
THE *BREVARD NEWS*
OCTOBER 9, 1903

HARVEY WASHINGTON WILEY

CHEMIST

1844–1930

Arlington National Cemetery, Arlington, Virginia

A Civil War veteran and Harvard graduate, Harvey Washington Wiley was a leading advocate of the Pure Food Movement of the early 1900s. Until the late 1800s, most food was grown or produced adjacent to the communities that consumed them, and, as a result, available unprocessed at markets. With urban populations growing rapidly and the rail network in the United States making it possible for food to be grown farther from the consumer, chemists were often tasked with activities that we now find common in food production, such as adding preservatives, dyes, and colors to make the food appear fresher.

Many food manufacturers believed this gave certain producers an unfair advantage, and consumers grew wary of adulterated foods. Wiley campaigned against margarine and baking powder with alum (not as pure as traditional baking powder). His test kitchen became infamous as the home of the Poison Squad—a group of healthy young men tasked with consuming increasingly larger portions of common food additives until they got sick. Their first target was borax, a mineral often used to doctor rancid meat. Wiley placed the borax in butter, milk, and meat. One Christmas menu read "Apple Sauce. Borax. Soup. Borax. Turkey. Borax. Borax. Canned Stringed Beans. Sweet Potatoes. White Potatoes. Turnips. Borax. Chipped Beef. Cream Gravy. Cranberry Sauce. Celery. Pickles. Rice Pudding. Milk. Bread and Butter. Tea. Coffee. A Little Borax."

The Poison Squad also tested sulfuric acid, saltpeter, formaldehyde, and copper sulfate. Wiley's publicity stunts earned disapproval in Washington but national public interest and support for his proposed Pure Food and Drug Act. By specifically targeting adulterated whiskeys, the act attracted firm support from makers of "straight whiskey" like Edmund H. Taylor, who championed the type of whiskey that was being made in Kentucky—which is to say, the old-fashioned, laborious kind, as opposed to that produced by commercial rectifiers and members of the Whiskey Trust, which operated large processing facilities in Indiana and Illinois. Rectifiers often added their own adulterations, including beading oil (glycerin), wood shavings, burnt sugar, prune juice, and creosote (for imitation Scotch). Wiley's collaboration with Taylor and other Kentucky distillers may have saved the reputation of American whiskey (though it didn't stop the tide of temperance. Wiley's book *Beverages and Their Adulteration* from 1907 is a great overview of whiskey history and science—very little has changed since then.

Before he left the Department of Chemistry, a forerunner to the FDA, Wiley seized a shipment of forty barrels and twenty kegs of Coca-Cola, claiming the product was poisonous (it contained caffeine, which Wiley disapproved of) and misleadingly labeled (no cocaine—the formula had changed, but the name remained). The resulting kerfuffle played out in Coca-Cola's favor, but caffeine was thereafter listed as a potentially harmful ingredient and must now be listed with ingredients.

In 1912, Wiley started working for *Good Housekeeping* magazine, and married a suffragette half his age. He died at home in 1930.

CHARLES LEDOWSKY

**WIRES FOR UNDERTAKER; KILLS SELF
ACCUSED DISTILLERY OFFICIAL
COMMITS SUICIDE ON TRAIN.
BY ASSOCIATED PRESS.**

CHICAGO, JAN. 20—*Charles Ledowsky, president of the Fox River Distilling Company of Chicago, whose name has been mentioned in connection with alleged forged warehouse receipts of R.E. Wathen & Company of Louisville, committed suicide by shooting today on a railroad train entering Chicago. Ledowsky was on a Michigan Central train from Syracuse. He telegraphed ahead to a Chicago undertaker, requesting him to meet the train and take his body, as he intended to do away with himself. An involuntary petition in bankruptcy was filed. Attorney Sidney Stein, representing Ledowsky's creditors, stated that Ledowsky had confessed to him that he had forged warehouse receipts for whisky valued at $250,000 or $300,000 and disposed of them through banks which he victimized.*

MARY WAZENIAK

MOONSHINER

CA. 1890–UNKNOWN

Lived in Chicago area; Interment unknown

Mary Wazeniak ran a speakeasy in Brookfield, Illinois, near Chicago. One evening, in 1923, George L. Rheaton, of LaGrange, Indiana, bought five or six shots of Mary's moonshine. He staggered out of the bar, walked about two hundred feet, and fell dead. Chemical analysis during an autopsy indicated that Rheaton died of methanol poisoning. "Moonshine Mary," as the press dubbed her, was thirty-four years old and a mother of three when she was sentenced to a year to life.

This is what we know of Mary. It's not much. And to read this, you would think that it was Mary who poisoned Rheaton, but it wasn't. It was the federal government.

By the mid-1920s, Prohibition's noble experiment was starting to show great wear on the people for whom it was meant to benefit. Still, alcohol was not that hard to find, as industrial alcohol is a necessary ingredient in aftershave, antifreeze, felt hats, embalming fluid, and fuel. Recognizing this temptation, and as a deterrence, the government routinely altered the chemical composition of the spirit to make it unpotable. The added chemical was methanol, which in trace quantities is present in all fermented beverages and in most distilled spirits—it's a simpler alcohol molecule, sometimes called wood alcohol—but in concentrated form is highly toxic. As little as thirty milliliters of methanol can blind a person; sixty milliliters is lethal. The federal government, in its wisdom, decided to add methanol to ethanol (the chemical we drink) so that it couldn't be consumed safely.

And yet methanol has a slightly lower boiling point than ethanol, and some enterprising moonshiners reasoned that the two could be separated through distillation. This is technically true, but difficult in practice, especially at the scale of a bootlegger using copper pots as small as ten gallons. Inevitably, methanol contaminated the ethanol, and people frequently got sick.

Over the Christmas holiday in 1926, for instance, twenty-three people died from methanol poisoning in New York City. The medical examiner, Charles Norris, spoke out against what he called a "national experiment in extermination." Government officials at the time—and many historians today—explain away such deaths as inevitable, given the country's ravenous appetite for spirits. But most of the deaths were avoidable. Imagine today's government, in an effort to reduce drug use, spraying marijuana crops with poison.

These days, people still fear homemade alcohol as something that might blind or kill the drinker. But if it is made from properly fermented sugars, there's no reason to expect moonshine to contain anything higher than ten parts per million of methanol. This is five to six times *less* than most commercial alcohol. You would have to drink north of thirty gallons of moonshine to get a harmful dose of methanol, and would die from the ethanol long before that became a possibility.

Mary Wazeniak in court

Confiscated moonshine stills in Oregon during Prohibition

OLD REVENUE AGENT KILLED

He Is Shot in Early Morning Attack on Lexington Distillery.

Special to The New York Times.

LEXINGTON. Ky.. Dec. 2.—William B. Anderson, aged 58, one of the oldest revenue men of the South, was shot dead this morning in a gun fight with whisky bandits at the James E. Pepper distillery in the west end of Lexington. Fully twenty-five shots were fired. Anderson was shot through the heart. Other watchmen on duty with Anderson fired at the robbers, whose bullets in return made hits visible today on the sides of the big warehouses, which contain 13,000 cases and 2,000 barrels of whisky of an estimated value of nearly a million dollars.

Anderson and his fellow guards were attacked from the darkness by two parties of thieves. The leader called out " Throw up your hands! " Anderson fired at this man. Then from two directions came a volley of shots. Anderson fell, while other guards pumped shot after shot at the bandits, who at first returned the fire and then fled in the darkness.

William B. Anderson
THE *NEW YORK TIMES*,
DECEMBER 3, 1920

Fire at Owensboro Distillery, 1960

In 1965, a tornado ripped the side off a warehouse at the J. T. S. Brown distillery (Wild Turkey)

HARRY BAKER

KILL RUM RUNNER.
ANOTHER WOUNDED IN BATTLE WITH FEDERAL
AGENTS AT LOUISVILLE FRIDAY

LOUISVILLE, K., JULY 28—*Federal agents killed Harry Baker, former lieutenant of police, and wounded another alleged rum runner during a gun fight here this morning at a distillery near the business section of the city. The alleged rum-runner intentionally drove their truck laden with 25 barrels of whiskey into a federal agent's automobile, then opened fire with pistols. The ten government agents returned the fire, killing Baker and wounding another. A third man was captured. The four escaped. Baker's accomplice, it was reported by hospital attachés, will probably die.*

GEORGE
REMUS

PHARMACIST,
LAWYER,
BOOTLEGGER

1876–1952
———

Riverside Cemetery,
Falmouth, Kentucky

IMOGENE
REMUS

BOOTLEGGER,
DISTILLERY
OWNER

1888–1927
———

Rosehill Cemetery,
Chicago, Illinois

G eorge Remus is the most underappreciated figure in American history.

Remus was the largest American bootlegger in the early days of Prohibition. He was the inspiration for *The Great Gatsby*. His daughter was a silent-film star. At one point, Remus owned most of the distilleries in the United States. He went to jail for his bootlegging and while in prison his wife started sleeping with the Prohibition agent assigned to his case. The two began systematically stripping Remus of his fortune, in particular his distilleries, while he was stuck in jail. When Remus got out, he hunted down his wife and shot her in broad daylight in a public park, then defended himself at trial, and got *himself exonerated*, arguing one of the country's first successful temporary insanity defenses.

Why have we been subjected to so many movies about Al Capone and Eliot Ness when Remus was certainly more psychologically compelling—not as a gangster, but as a slightly dishonest businessman trying to make his way in America through a conviction in his own ability to persuade? Remus bootlegged because he liked money, not booze, and because, though he knew the law, he disagreed with it. He believed Prohibition to be an injustice, a legally untenable overreach of federal power. To him, the only moral truth was that which could be argued in a court of law, and, in the eyes of the unjustly denied dry populace, a jury of his peers, he was a moral crusader. How quintessentially American! George Remus, fat and bald, with no interest in drinking, finds injustice and opportunity in Prohibition and steers it to his enormous financial advantage, only to let hubris and love derail him. The difference between a Remus and a Bronfman (see page 188) is thin as paper, but separates the dynasty from the disgraced.

Remus emigrated from Germany with his parents when he was a boy, moving first to Baltimore for a short time and eventually Chicago. He got a job as a clerk in an uncle's drugstore, went to pharmacy school, and bought the business from his uncle. Still, Remus dreamed of more, and went to law school. By 1900, he had his own practice set up in the Ashland Block building, a modern office tower designed by Daniel Burnham, and a prestigious address shared by famed attorney Clarence Darrow and poet Edgar Lee Masters.

Remus gained early notoriety from the defense of William Cheney Ellis, who shot his wife in the chest and head, slit her throat, and then made a feeble attempt to kill himself. Hotel security found him wearing his wife's kimono and smoking a cigar, visibly distraught. He confessed to the crime, and indeed had written letters to his children and made calls warning family and friends what he intended to do. Ellis pled not guilty. Remus, confronted with what appeared to be an open-and-shut case, proposed a defense of temporary insanity, an argument that would fail in this case but establish Remus's reputation as a creative defender, willing to test the limits of legal interpretation in the interest of both his clients and his own renown.

He also applied his imagination to Prohibition law. When the ban went into effect in 1920, Remus sensed an opportunity through a legal loophole. Before Prohibition, when a distiller entered a barrel into a warehouse, he was given a receipt from the government that could be used to redeem the barrel, at which time the tax had to be paid. Distillers, in advance of Prohibition, were sitting on millions of barrels in inventory—or, to be more specific, millions of receipts for barrels in government custody. Remus, anticipating that medicinal whiskey would become a practical loophole for drinkers, started buying up receipts in order to distribute the whiskey as medicine. Prohibition made it illegal to buy whiskey, but not receipts for whiskey barrels, provided one could bottle it as medicinal whiskey. Remus, after all, had gone to pharmacy school and was licensed to distribute medicine. "I was impressed by the rapidity with which those men, without any brains at all, piled up fortunes in the liquor business," Remus once recalled. "The more I studied the Volstead Act, the more I was convinced of its frailties, and so I decided to get in on the ground floor, strike while the iron was hot."

On the eve of Prohibition, Remus was also facing some personal difficulty. He had married his first wife, Lillian, in 1899, and the two were raising their daughter, Romola, who, in 1908 was the first actress to portray Dorothy in a filmed adaptation of *The Wizard of Oz*. Despite this excitement at home, however, Remus was restless. He ran into Imogene Holmes, recently divorced, working in an Evanston delicatessen, where he frequently bought his groceries. He went out of his way to pick them up personally, stopping to chat with Imogene; she went to work for him at his law office, and they began an affair.

In 1919, Remus and Lillian got divorced, and Remus married Imogene and moved to Cincinnati, then one of the most fashionable cities in the country. More important, Cincinnati was within a three-hundred-mile radius of nearly every government whiskey warehouse in the country. Remus bought a mansion in the elegant district Price Hill and furnished it accordingly; he began construction on an Olympic-size Grecian indoor pool, as he and Imogene were both fond of swimming. Remus also built two tunnels under the house, both to store whiskey and as a possible getaway. He also kept a stable for his racing Thoroughbreds, and a farm on the outskirts of town, which became known colloquially as the Death Valley Farm.

Remus purchased two drug companies in New York City and arranged for legal services and connections to federal agents who could grant permits for withdrawals from bonded warehouses. He bought the Squibb distillery, in Lawrenceburg, Indiana; the Rugby distillery in Louisville; the Hill and Hill distillery in Owensboro; and the Burks Spring distillery in Loretto (which now produces Maker's Mark). Within a few years, he had an interest in Jack Daniel's whiskey (whose barrels were now based in Saint Louis), the Pogue distillery in Maysville, and the Edgewood distillery in Cincinnati; he had his sights on the Fleischmann distillery. At one point, Remus owned fourteen distilleries in all, and was making, by one estimate, up to twenty-five million dollars annually, or close to four hundred million in today's dollars. He did this by selling medicinal liquor, robbing his own trucks carrying medicinal liquor, and bribing nearly everyone in the supply chain of police and political oversight to keep quiet.

Remus's transition from lawyer with an interest in bending Prohibition law to full-fledged bootlegger could probably be traced to the moment when he bribed Jess Smith, a mysterious functionary within the U.S. Department of Justice of Warren Harding's fantastically corrupt cabinet. Smith and Attorney General Harry Daugherty had grown up together and were very closely linked throughout their lives. (They lived together in many instances.) Smith was known for giving advice on ladies' fashion, and was particularly close to Florence (Flossie) Harding. Smith and other members of Harding's political entourage often partied at a "little green house on K Street," as it would be known. Remus paid Smith at least fifty thousand dollars for immunity from federal prosecution, and this figure would grow to two hundred fifty thousand in later tellings.

In 1923, Remus threw a party. He already had a reputation for throwing good parties. He was known to put hundred-dollar bills under the dinner plates of guests. At one party, each guest got a gold-engraved Elgin watch. But the party in 1923 was certainly one of the greatest in the history of parties. Remus bought the stock of a bankrupt Cincinnati jeweler and gave away the store to his guests: diamond rings for the women, tie clasps for the men. Imogene appeared in an elaborately staged swimming routine, wearing a revealing bathing suit. As the party was winding down, guests were invited to the lawn, where the women in attendance were presented with 1923 Pontiacs. Meanwhile, Remus, sober as always, had slipped away long before, retiring to his library to eat a bowl of ice cream and read a biography of Abraham Lincoln.

Later that same year, Smith either committed suicide or was murdered; shortly after that, Harding himself died of exhaustion, food poisoning, or murder, depending on who is telling the tale. (After Harding's death, Flossie went home to the White House and started scouring

A pool party at the Remus mansion

Harding's office, burning every file she could find in an attempt to protect his reputation.) Remus was suddenly without an ally in government, and within months he was sentenced to two years in the Atlanta penitentiary. He signed over power of attorney to his wife, so that she could continue to run his business interests while he was in prison.

By 1925, Mabel Walker Willebrandt, an assistant attorney general also known as the "First Lady of the Law," had been hearing rumors of corruption in the Atlanta federal penitentiary. She sent in one of her favorite agents, Franklin Dodge, to investigate. Ironically, Remus had heard of Dodge from another inmate, who thought he might be favorable to Remus and could help him get out early. He wrote to Imogene and suggested that she contact him.

She did, and she was immediately taken with Dodge. Tall and handsome, he seemed nearly irresistible. She met with him at the Atlanta penitentiary while on a visit to Remus, and by one account the two were intimate in the prison, using the warden's office as a love nest while her husband sat behind bars elsewhere in the building.

Remus was facing serious legal troubles, and it seemed that even if he could get out on parole, he might face deportation on a technicality, or prosecution on other minor charges. To make matters worse, Imogene was using her power of attorney to strip Remus of his assets. Dodge and

Imogene began selling warehouse receipts, essentially profiting off of business arrangements that Dodge uncovered as a federal investigator. Imogene herself was under scrutiny at the time, regarding the illegal removal of barrels from the Jack Daniel warehouse. Press reports about Dodge put Willebrandt in a tricky position, and she forced him to resign, though he was never indicted or censured for his actions. When the dust settled, Dodge and Imogene had done their worst. They sold the Fleischmann distillery for eighty-one thousand dollars, and Imogene sent Remus one hundred dollars for his share; she then filed for divorce. In the following days, she and Dodge would begin systematically selling Remus's distilleries to anyone who would buy, at any price. She also sold Remus's collection of Washington and Lincoln memorabilia, including a rare signature of Washington valued at three thousand dollars.

Remus realized his best shot at permanent freedom was cooperation. As the Jack Daniel's case went to trial, Remus entered witness protection and was placed in custody at the same hotel in Indianapolis where Imogene and Dodge were staying. Remus saw Dodge in the lobby and ran to confront him, but was restrained by an associate before he could attack.

At the start of Imogene's trial, the government sensed that Remus's testimony against her could be perceived as motivated by vengeance, and, deciding that the case had become too risky, called off the trial. This freeing of Imogene deprived Remus of his public vindication, though he took some solace in the fact that Congressman Fiorello La Guardia, fervently opposed to Prohibition, had begun an investigation of Dodge and Imogene as an example of the depravity associated with corrupt government officials and craven bootleggers.

Remus went off to serve a year in the state penitentiary on nuisance charges. When he got out, he returned to his Price Hill mansion to find the doors nailed shut and windows boarded up. He had to break into his own house, whereupon he found it stripped of its furnishings and artworks—even the chandeliers had been taken. He wept.

The day that Remus was to go to court to finalize his divorce with Imogene, he instructed his driver to go over to the hotel where she

George Remus in jail, 1927

was staying. He saw Imogene and her daughter Ruth getting into a taxi. Imogene, noticing Remus, instructed her taxi driver to evade him. So began a car chase, with Remus and his driver forcing Imogene's car to the curb at the edge of Eden Park. Remus got out of the car, but as he did, Imogene's taxi drove over the curb and sped away, and the chase was back on. Finally, near the reservoir, Imogene got out of the taxi and ran up a hill. Remus chased her, shouting and swearing as he ran. Eventually he grabbed her by the wrist, pulled out his gun, and shot her in the stomach. Then he dropped her to the ground, still screaming, and ran into the woods. Ruth, who had witnessed the whole confrontation, comforted Imogene and got her to a hospital, but it was too late. Remus turned himself in to police later that day.

Remus opted to serve as his own counsel at trial. He had a tough road, as he had confessed to the killing in broad daylight in a public park. He recalled the case of Harry Thaw, who had killed the architect and "serial seducer of teenage girls" Stanford White in a fit of jealous rage. Thaw pled temporary insanity—successfully. Remus saw an angle.

The trial lasted for a month, in December 1927. The prosecution managed to bungle the case, trying to prove a conspiracy that Remus killed Imogene to prevent her from testifying to Prohibition crimes. Conspiracy was harder to prove than murder, and the prosecution, led by President William Howard Taft's son, was not compelling. Though three expert medical doctors testified that Remus was sane, Remus turned his closing argument into an indictment of Prohibition. Referring to himself, Remus declared: "If this defendant goes down to oblivion, then it will be as a martyr to that awful mistake. Remus always sold good liquor. Never in the annals of criminology has one defendant been in nine different penal institutions for the violation of one law. This atrocious bit of legislation is making hypocrites of our judges, our prosecutors—of us all."

It took the jury nineteen minutes to acquit. One juror said they could have finished it in ten minutes and viewed the verdict as a Christmas gift. Oh, Remus!—fond of pinochle and Limburger-cheese -and-raw-onion sandwiches; competitive swimmer, teetotaler, presidential history buff, and confirmed disliker of underwear—he lived the rest of his days in a quiet life in northern Kentucky. He died in 1952.

During his glory days, Remus frequently stayed at the Seelbach Hotel in Louisville, Kentucky, while traveling for business. A young Francis Scott Key Fitzgerald also frequented the hotel, when on leave from military service from nearby Camp Taylor. (It is said that he had been thrown out for excessive enjoyment of alcohol.) In *The Great Gatsby*, his ingénue Daisy marries Tom Buchanan at the Muhlbach Hotel in Louisville, an obvious stand-in for the Seelbach. The possibility for coincidence has long fueled the speculation that Gatsby was based on Remus. Though the two were probably not in the hotel at the same time, a meeting wouldn't be necessary. Remus was already in newspaper headlines associated with his bootlegging in 1922, about the time the young writer moved to Great Neck, New York, to write about a former pharmacist from Louisville in a shady business who throws lavish parties and whose great love derails him. *The Great Gatsby* was published in 1925, two years before Remus killed his wife. One could argue that if Gatsby was based on Remus, maybe Remus was, in part, based on Gatsby.

A TOUR OF CINCINNATI

CINCINNATI WAS ONCE the most fashionable cities in the United States, and its location, surrounded by fields of grain with proximity to railroads and the Ohio River, made it a hub of distilling until Prohibition.

1. HILLFOREST
Thomas Gaff's mansion in Aurora, Indiana, now open as a National Historic Landmark, his distillery is now a microbrewery

2. SEAGRAM DISTILLERY
Now called MGP of Indiana, formerly owned by Samuel Bronfman's Seagram

3. SQUIBB DISTILLERY
Started by Squibb, and run for many years by Lew Rosenstiel of Schenley, now abandoned

4. GREENDALE CEMETERY
Final resting place of William P. Squibb

5. WILLIAM HENRY HARRISON
President for a month, Indian-conflict general, former distiller, and later advocate for temperance

6. FLEISCHMANN DISTILLERY
Charles Louis Fleischmann opened a distillery here in Riverside but after Remus and others gutted its inventory during Prohibition

7. THOMAS GAFF
Disitller, financier, steamboat builder, is buried in Spring Grove Cemetery

8. CHARLES FLEISCHMANN
Presided over an empire of distilleries, yeast, breakfast cereal, banks, and other enterprises; son Louis, mayor of Cincinnati, is also buried here

9. JOHN A. ROEBLING BRIDGE
Built in 1866, this historic suspension bridge was a precursor to the Brooklyn Bridge, also designed by Roebling, a French engineer

10. LEWIS ROSENSTIEL
Distiller and owner of many brands after Prohibition with his company Schenley

11. EDEN PARK GAZEBO
Location where George Remus shot and killed his wife, Imogene, in broad daylight

12. SIDNEY FRANK
Importer of Jägermeister, creator of Grey Goose, son-in-law of Lewis Rosenstiel

13. GEORGE REMUS
Lawyer, bootlegger, and murderer, is buried in Falmouth, Kentucky, about forty miles south of Cincinnati

TO INDIANAPOLIS

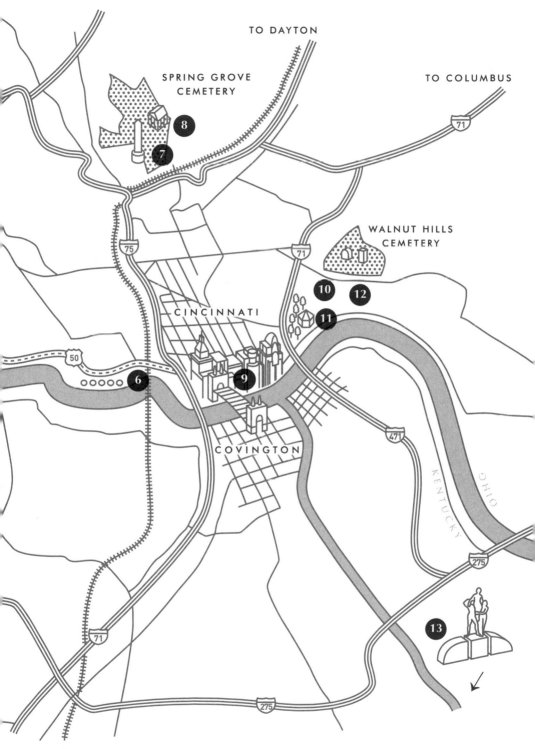

TO DAYTON

SPRING GROVE
CEMETERY

TO COLUMBUS

71

8

7

75

71

WALNUT HILLS
CEMETERY

10   12

CINCINNATI   11

50

6   9

COVINGTON

471

KENTUCKY   OHIO

275

71

13

275

TO LEXINGTON

Think Family Was Slain And Then House Ignited To Cover Trace of Crime

International News Service

CONFLUENCE, Nov. 27.—The re-covery of four remaining bodies from the ruins of the farmhouse of Sam-uel Russo, near here, where nine per-sons were burned to death yesterday, dded further mystery to the case to-day when an autopsy revealed that all the bodies were headless. That the bodies were decapitated and the building fired to cover the crime was the theory on which police were working today.

A bootlegger's war, which before had taken a toll of one life in this district, is believed to have been re-sponsible for the murder. Further killings were anticipated as Russo's friends became organized for re-venge.

Firemen claim the construction of the house, with ample exits, pre-cludes a possibility that the mem-bers of the family might have been trapped by the flames.

Samuel Russo and Eight Others
THE CONFLUENCE *EVENING NEWS*,
NOVEMBER 27, 1923

JOSEPH GALLO

MOONSHINER

1882–1933

St. Stanislaus Cemetery, Modesto, California

Born in Italy in 1882, Giuseppe "Joseph" Gallo moved to California and started a wine company under the family name in 1906 with his brother Mike, buying and reselling bulk wine from small vineyards. Mike was a small-time hustler and went to prison for a failed swindle when his protection money to local cops exposed a ring of corruption. Once out of prison, Mike had his brother Joe run a small distillery in his barn on his Livermore ranch, making whiskey and brandy with the help of Joe's sons, Ernest and Julio, who often kept watch over the still.

In 1933, Joseph and his wife, Assunta, were found shot to death on their farm in Fresno. Assunta, who went by Susie, had been shot in the back of the head in the yard while she was feeding the pigs; Joseph had been shot in front of a mirror, in an alcove of the dining room.

Ernest, Joseph's son, said that his father had become despondent over financial difficulties. No fingerprints were found that could have corroborated the claim of murder-suicide, but no inquest was held. A sixty-dollar tax payment was found in the mailbox, which called into question the financial troubles, but ill health was also sourced as a potential woe. No sign of struggle was found.

Joseph's sons, who were deep enough in bootlegging to do business directly with Al Capone, were suspected of the crime, but they overcame this suspicion to form one of the most successful winemaking enterprises of the twentieth century, focused primarily on inexpensive brands like Carlo Rossi, Boone's Farm, Bartles & Jaymes, Barefoot Cellars, Turning Leaf, and spirits such as E&J brandies and New Amsterdam vodka. At one point, according to the *New York Times*, more than half of the California grape harvest made its way into Gallo products.

AL CAPONE

BOOTLEGGER, GANGSTER

1899–1947

Mount Carmel Cemetery, Chicago, Illinois

Alphonse Gabriel Capone was born in Brooklyn at 95 Navy Street, an address that today is an on-ramp to the Brooklyn-Queens Expressway. While the neighborhood had once been predominantly Irish in the second half of the 1800s (see Clinton Gilbert, page 71), by the turn of the century, it was more eclectic. Capone was born to Italian immigrants, his father a barber and his mother a seamstress. He had eight brothers and sisters, two of whom would work for him in later years.

At fourteen, Capone was expelled from his Catholic school for hitting a female teacher in the face. It is speculated that he contracted syphilis by patronizing the brothels that lined Sands Street in the 1910s. In those days, the neighborhood was dominated by street gangs, notably the Bowery Boys and the Five Points Gang. In his teens, Capone was employed by Frankie Yale at a nightclub called the Harvard Inn on Coney Island, and, after flirting with the girlfriend of Frank Galluccio, got his face slashed by Galluccio, leading to the nickname Scarface.

Capone married, and fathered a son shortly before moving to Chicago, in 1920. He became the most notorious bootlegger and gangster in America, emblematic of the failures and dangers of Prohibition law. Indicted for tax evasion, in 1931, he was convicted and sentenced. After being transferred from Atlanta and imprisoned in the new federal penitentiary on Alcatraz Island from 1934 to 1939, he moved to Florida. He eventually died of complications of syphilis, gonorrhea, and chronic drug addiction in Miami Beach.

Al Capone at a court appearance

GERTRUDE CECILIA LYTHGOE

LIQUOR WHOLESALER, RUM RUNNER

1888–1974

Died Los Angeles, California; Interment unknown

Gertrude Lythgoe was born in Bowling Green, Ohio, and when she was very young, her family suffered three tragedies: Her father's glass factory burned, her sister went deaf, and her mother died. Sent to live in an orphanage, she eventually succeeded in school in Indianapolis while trying to make it as a singer at night.

She spent time in San Francisco, Hawaii, London, and New York, working in the importing business before a risky bet on the stock market put her at the mercy of an old employer, who sent her to the Bahamas to work the wholesale alcohol trade and try to capitalize on being the nearest wet point to a dry land.

There, she became the first woman to get a wholesaler's license and set up shop carrying whiskey—mostly Haig's & McTavish's Scotch, but sometimes American whiskey, which was more popular. In the early days, there was a flood of money as ships would arrive, stock up, and head out for further distribution. Nassau, Havana, and Tampico, Mexico, became boomtowns where bootleggers paid for cargo in large bills, creating a manic atmosphere on small islands.

Lythgoe had an exotic look and endured the constant speculation from strangers as to her ethnicity. She had a British father and a Scottish mother, but she was confused for Spanish, American Indian, Russian, Egyptian, or Gypsy. Lythgoe encouraged the confusion and seemed elusive to many who knew her. The proprietor of the Lucerne Hotel, whom Lythgoe knew as "Mother," at one point said she looked like Cleopatra, and the name stuck, probably to Lythgoe's delight, though by that point, she was already going by Grace as often as Gertrude.

Lythgoe's business in liquor aroused suspicion. She was thought a spy, and generally viewed with wariness. Lythgoe was cagey about many of her activities, though she asserted she never broke the law, even after targeted by American detectives.

Still, she wrote a memoir of her time bootlegging, and while it lacks detail about the particulars of her business, it is rich and colorful with life in Nassau during Prohibition as a single woman trying to run a business. There are episodes with creepy men, gossiping competitors, sexist liquor board administrators, and customers with terrible taste:

> The Lucerne was now crowded with buyers and their crews. With my samples I approached each buyer. One would taste, another would test, pouring a few drops on the palm of each hand, rubbing his hands together, passing them in front of his nose to sniff the aroma. Others would "stretch" the whiskey by mixing it with water to see how long the color and taste would remain. Others used the tincture-of-iron text. After all these performances, some would pronounce the goods "wonderful." "Well, it just hasn't the kick," others would say.

She linked up with Captain Bill McCoy, the "real McCoy," whose reputable goods gave history the idiom for any genuine article. They embarked on a trip to Rum Row, where liquor-laden ships lined up near New York City, just inside international waters, to sell whiskey, rum, and gin to bootleggers bold enough to hazard the trip past the revenue agency's cutters. She off-loaded her rye, and on a trip back to London, inadvertently gave her story to H. de Winton Wigley, a journalist in disguise, who published her story in the *London Daily News*.

From then on, the press couldn't help but be fascinated with Lythgoe, who was dubbed "Queen of the Bahamas" and painted so broadly that any representation seems more a fantastical projection of the times than any specific account of the real Lythgoe. She represented something broader about her era: When women in the United States were only recently allowed to vote, here was a woman running a complicated, illicit (and, by all accounts, successful) business when American society was trapped in a cultural inflection point, at once deeply conservative and progressive.

Of course, there was plenty of backlash. Mary A. Sullivan of the women's division of the New York City Police Department didn't believe in women bootleggers, because they weren't strong enough to load and unload trucks. Another article accused Lythgoe of staging photographs and exaggerating her stories, suggesting that once she was at sea, she "threw herself down on the deck, screamed, and had to be taken back to shore. A case of cold feet." The article also called her "an awful little coward." It seems the writer's source in the revenue agency offered the spin that, in hindsight, shows a desperately embarrassed agency more willing to propagate libel than concede their own deep failures.

In 1925, Lythgoe was arrested in Miami for smuggling whiskey into New Orleans, though she claimed the whiskey was stolen and was eventually exonerated. She left rum and settled in Detroit, eventually getting into the rental car business. She died in Los Angeles in 1974.

"Cleo" Lythgoe with rum runner Bill McCoy on his boat, *Tomoka*

RUM VAT WHERE SLAIN MAN WAS FOUND

Unknown Moonshiner
THE *BROOKLYN DAILY EAGLE*,
JULY 18, 1929

BIRDIE BROWN

MOONSHINER

1871–1933

Lewistown City Cemetery, Lewiston, Montana

Birdie Brown was a homesteader from Missouri who moved to Montana in 1898 hoping to start a new life along Brickyard Creek in Fergus County. She grew wheat, oats, and barley and kept a modest cabin with incredible views of the Judith Mountains where the prairie starts to give way to the Northern Rockies. Her company on the property was chickens and a black cat.

Brown kept odd jobs to make money, one of which was dry cleaning. She also made moonshine, which was revered throughout the county in an era when good liquor was hard to find anywhere, and especially in the remote parts of the country. Being a single black woman on the frontier was probably not easy in the early 1900s, but Brown made whiskey, and that earned her a lot of friends and goodwill.

This also made it hard for her to keep a low profile, and in 1933, just before the end of Prohibition, a revenue officer came out to her house to warn her about illegal distilling. Perhaps flustered, she momentarily ignored her dry cleaning and moonshine still, and the gasoline she was using for dry cleaning caught fire and exploded in her face.

Brown died of her injuries that day. There are reports that a black cat still stands guard at her abandoned homestead.

Illegal stills in a Brookyn apartment, 1927

Exploding Still Said to Have Caused Death of Factory Workmen

TOLEDO, O. — (P) — Four bodies were taken from the ruins of the Carl Weber Manufacturing company plant here early today after a series of explosions in the building were followed by fire. The explosions shattered the second story of the brick building and blew out a wall.

The bodies of the four persons were not identified at once. The first estimate of the building damage was $15,000. The cause has not been determined. Search for additional bodies was begun at once.

Firemen said they found evidences of a large distilling layout in the building, including two large stills, two 550 gallon tanks, 300 one-gallon cans and an assortment of copper tanks and tubing.

An explossion of a still caused the fire, Richard Lawler, district fire chief, said.

Four Unnamed Distillers
THE *TOLEDO DAILY MESSENGER*,
SEPTEMBER 22, 1930

MARY
DOWLING

DISTILLERY OWNER,
BOOTLEGGER,
BUSINESSWOMAN

1859–1930

Lawrenceburg Cemetery,
Lawrenceburg, Kentucky

JOSEPH
L.
BEAM

DISTILLER

1868–1956

Burdstown City Cemetery,
Bardstown, Kentucky

W hile most of the women in this book who were distillers tended to work illegally, Mary Dowling is one of the few who ran a legitimate distillery—and did some bootlegging on the side, for good measure.

Mary was born in Kentucky to Irish immigrants. She married John Dowling, an Irish immigrant himself, in 1875. He eventually partnered with the Waterfill & Frazier distillery, a popular brand of whiskey during and after the Civil War. He helped quadruple the distillery's capacity, increased its barrel storage, and modernized the warehouses. He eventually became full owner of the distillery and, perhaps recognizing that his legacy was at stake, brought his wife into the business at a crucial time, before he died at age sixty-one.

Mary was a good steward of the business, rebuilding after a fire and helping to found a local bank with capital from her business. But Prohibition would close her doors. She removed many barrels from her warehouse, hoping to salvage as much of her future as she could, but in 1924, informant bootleggers brought revenue agents into her shuttered distillery, where they found six thousand quart jars of illegally bottled whiskey.

People were entitled to build up large reserves of spirits in advance of Prohibition, as the "21" Club in New York City had famously done, and this was Dowling's argument. Still, she and her sons were convicted, though when officials found the trial stenographer's notes to be illegible, the convictions were overturned.

Dowling took this second chance. She disassembled her distillery and relocated it to Juarez, Mexico, just over the border from El Paso. She hired Joseph L. Beam to run the distillery, and many of his sons learned the business there. Since she couldn't afford to build warehouses in a short time, the barrels were laid out to age in rows on the sand, surrounded by a high fence. She was sure that Prohibition would be repealed and wanted to have supply when the time came.

Interestingly, some of Dowling's old whiskey from the Kentucky distillery had been sold to Julian Van Winkle, who had a medicinal license. Van Winkle wrote her a letter expressing annoyance that her Mexican whiskey was competing with what he was trying to sell, causing him some grief. Of course, any quantity of the Mexican whiskey sold in the United States would have been illegal, but empires would be built on this illegal traffic.

Joseph L. had seven sons who all became distillers and were influential in the industry: Elmo worked at Maker's Mark, Roy worked at Stitzel-Weller, and so on, and so forth. Joseph's wife, Katherine, was the sister of William McGill, master distiller at Stitzel-Weller for many years.

Dowling died in 1930 and never got to see the yield from her premonition of repeal. Her sons weren't able to continue to grow the business, and eventually the distillery and brand were sold. It is owned today by Heaven Hill but is not in active production. One gets the sense that if she had lived just a few more years, the fortunes of Dowling's brand and her distillery may have been radically different.

FRANK W. KNIGHT

REVENUE COLLECTOR

DIED 1918

Interment unknown

F rank W. Knight, a revenue collector from Cary, North Carolina, hoped to catch and apprehend the notorious illicit distiller Ed Harmon in the hills of North Carolina in 1918. Knight and three other deputies descended on an illicit still near the town of Kennebec, while Harmon was in the midst of operating his still. Gunfight broke out. "Harmon stood his ground, firing upon Knight and breaking his thigh and wounding him in his arm in two places," the *Charlotte Observer* reported. "Knight died from a blood clot caused by the wounds."

Later, Harmon would be shot (not mortally), captured, and convicted, though he had "openly boasted that no man could take him alive. He went armed with rifle and pistol, slept in a different place every night, as a general terror to a large scope of country, and was understood to be the backer of several large distilleries." Harmon's legacy was secure, though. "He was so shrewd and wary that he was known as the 'wild turkey.'"

Parker and Earl Beam supervise the filling of fermenters at Heaven Hill in Bardstown

THE *MUSKOGEE TIMES-DEMOCRAT*,

JANUARY 13, 1923

B. M. HUFFAKER

ARREST IN DISTILLERY MURDER

LAWRENCEBURG, KY., JAN 13 — *With Clarence Satterly, 21, under arrest in connection with the slaying of B. M. Huffaker, 60, guard at the Old Joe Distillery here, officials today declared the mystery surrounding the murder of the veteran government employee Thursday night practically was cleared up. Satterly was taken to Lexington for safe keeping last night.*

The Old Joe Distillery, abandoned during Prohibition

PARKER LLOYD SEAY

MOONSHINER AND NASCAR PIONEER

1919–1941

Dawsonville Cemetery, Dawsonville, Georgia

Junior Johnson gets a lot of credit for turning a career as a moonshine runner into a career as a NASCAR driver, and much of that credit is due to a profile by Tom Wolfe in *Esquire*, cleverly titled "The Last American Hero is Junior Johnson. Yes!" But it was another driver, Lloyd Seay (pronounced "See"), who was just as deserving—or at least would have been, had his life not been cut short in 1941 during a dispute over sugar, seven years before NASCAR was founded.

Seay never learned to read and write, but he tinkered with cars, drove fast, and ran moonshine to Atlanta twice a day. "Lanky, blond, and youthful," as the Greenwood, South Carolina, *Index-Journal* described him. Seay got his start at Lakewood Park in Atlanta, then a dirt track made from red Georgia clay. A story goes that he got pulled over by the highway patrol and offered the cop twenty dollars. The cop said, "Hell, Lloyd, the fine ain't but ten dollars," to which Lloyd replied, "I know it, but I ain't gonna have time to stop next time. I'm payin' in advance."

By 1941, Seay had already won two races at High Point, after which the paper dubbed him the "daredevil of the dusty roads." He set a track record for driving sixty miles an hour for seventy-five miles. Seay rolled his car *twice* at Daytona and still finished first. In his next Daytona start, he began in fifteenth place and led all fifty laps. At his last race, he missed qualifying, started in last place, and won, taking the purse of $450.

After the win, Seay stayed with his brother Jim. A cousin, Woodrow Anderson, came over to settle a dispute over a sack of sugar, which Seay had charged to his account, displeasing Woodrow. The three decided to head to an aunt's house to resolve the dispute, but stopped on the way at Woodrow's father's house to get water from the well for the radiator. Anderson warned Jim that if he didn't want to get mixed up in anything, he had better get out of the car. Jim refused, and Anderson pulled a gun out of the bib of his overalls and shot Jim through the neck; then he turned the gun on Seay and shot him in the heart. The altercation left Seay dead and his brother in critical condition. Woodrow was sentenced to life in prison.

Raymond Parks, an uncle of Seay and a NASCAR pioneer, who served time for hauling moonshine himself, had initially funded Seay and another nephew, Roy Hall, serving as a sort of "team owner" before racing was properly organized. Parks took Seay's death hard and bought him an extra-large tombstone that featured a relief of his racecar and his Lakewood trophy. Seay had raced under number seven for his entire career, except for his last race, when, for reasons unknown, he had painted on the number thirteen.

Lloyd Seay racing at Atlanta's Lakewood Speedway in 1941

I n Yiddish, *bronfn* means liquor, so perhaps it was fate that Samuel Bronfman would enter the liquor business. But first, Sam and his parents, along with a rabbi and two servants, moved from Russia to Saskatchewan, Canada, and later to Manitoba, with plans to farm tobacco. These dreams were made moot by the realities of the Canadian climate. Yechiel, Sam's father, took a number of odd jobs, including for the railway and in a sawmill. The family sold firewood and frozen whitefish, did some horse trading (of course), and eventually, in 1903, got into the hotel business, which Sam quickly discovered was really the liquor business. Furthermore, the frontier of the Canadian prairie allowed for a certain freedom from scrutiny and the politics of Canadian temperance, which, like in the United States, was largely motivated by Protestant distaste for newer immigrants.

When Prohibition went into effect in the United States, Yechiel started shipping alcohol as a distributor, first buying the then useless stocks of American bourbon. In 1920, the Bronfmans imported three hundred thousand gallons of brands like Old Crow and Sunny Brook, diluted it with grain whiskey and water, and shipped it back across the border. This whiskey was consolidated in export houses, or "boozoriums," close to the American border; in collaboration with a label-printing company, buyers could create customized whiskeys in bulk. The business was soon selling twenty-six thousand cases a month, most of which was driven a few miles over the border and, from there, to points anywhere in the States. Though the boozoriums were technically legal, they were stocked with weapons, and Sam's brother-in-law Paul Matoff was killed by means of a shotgun blast through a window while counting money in a warehouse in Bienfait.

Canada was working through its own version of Prohibition in the early 1910s, and various provincial governments were taking control of liquor distribution. Sensing that distribution from Saskatchewan and Manitoba would no longer be tenable, and already making by one estimate about four hundred thousand dollars a month, the Bronfman family entered production by buying a defunct distillery in Louisville, Kentucky, and rebuilding it in Ville LaSalle, outside Montreal. The same year, in 1923, the family entered a partnership with the Distillery Company Limited, based in England, through which they bought malt whiskey in bulk and then blended it with grain spirit from their Coffey still in Ville LaSalle. They called the resulting product Old Highland whiskey, Prince of Wales, and other Scotchy-sounding names, and they distributed them through their export houses, though now they were operating on a larger scale. In 1928, the company bought a distillery from the Seagram family.

Joseph Seagram, born in 1841, had gotten into distilling by working as a bookkeeper in a gristmill and, later, a flour mill that had a side business in distilling; by 1883, he owned the mill outright and focused on the company's distilling business. In 1907, he created Seagram's VO, which would become one of the largest-selling whiskeys in history. Seagram loved racehorses, and imported mares from England. Seagram's horses won Canada's premier racing event, the Queen's Plate, eight consecutive years and fifteen times overall. However, with Seagram's death in 1919 and American Prohibition looming, Seagram's heirs were looking to sell. As for the Bronfman family, they thought, perhaps rightly, that a company called Seagram would sell more whiskey than a company called Bronfman.

The late 1920s were a strange time to be in the distillery business. Distillery owners who had been holding on to their factories in the hopes that Prohibition would end were finding it hard to maintain their resolve: The years ground on, owners died, interests shifted. Even those American distillers with medicinal licenses that allowed for continued operation often found it difficult to make money. At the same time, certain distillers, especially in Canada, were building a fortune. There was intense speculation after the fall of Prohibition as to whether the Bronfman family (and other Canadian distillers) sold their whiskey illegally to American bootleggers. One thing is certain: Americans would have their liquor, Prohibition or not, and anyone who could connect them to it stood to make a lot of money. By the end of the decade, Canadian distillers enjoyed a place of prominence—in terms of capital, product quality, and business infrastructure—that would continue long after Prohibition ended.

Bronfman marketed brands that had previously been established by Seagram: Calvert, Dewar's, and Seven Crown. And, over time, the company shed its association with bootlegging and diversified into other industries, notably oil and entertainment. Sam's daughter Phyllis became one of the great patrons of modern architecture, responsible for Mies van der Rohe's Seagram Tower on Park Avenue in New York City, one of the first modern skyscrapers, since copied endlessly around the world. Sam's son Edgar expanded the company through a series of deals for companies producing oil and chemicals. Sam died in 1971, and in 1993 Edgar ceded control to his son, Edgar Jr., who divested the company's stake in DuPont, a position his father fought hard to acquire, and bought MCA, which owned Universal and Polygram entertainment. With huge debts, the company foundered, and the remainder of Sam Bronfman's bootlegging empire was dismantled and sold off. Most of the liquor business went to Pernod Ricard and Diageo, the entertainment assets to Vivendi, and the soft drinks and mixers to Coca-Cola.

For a family obsessed with lineage, it is worth noting that Edgar Jr.'s son was briefly married to the Sri Lankan singer M.I.A.; their son was born in 2009, so we have some time until the next chapter in the Bronfman narrative is written.

JAMES
"JIM"
BEAUREGARD
BEAM

DISTILLER

1864–1947

Bardstown City Cemetery,
Bardstown, Kentucky

BOOKER
NOE

DISTILLER,
BRAND SPOKESMAN

1929–2004

Bardstown City Cemetery,
Bardstown, Kentucky

I n popular imagination, it's easy to lump Jim Beam in with Jack Daniel, Elijah Craig, and Evan Williams, all frontier distillers who became household names long after their deaths. In fact, Jim Beam is a relatively recent comer to the bourbon bottle, and though his family has a long history in distilling, Beam himself died in 1947, having carried the family business through two world wars and Prohibition, and was a modern distiller by contrast to most names that adorn whiskey bottles.

While the Beam family started distilling on Hardin's Creek in Manton, Kentucky, his branch of the family had a distillery just a few miles northwest of Bardstown, where it made a brand with the unlikely name of Old Tub. Jim and his brother-in-law reorganized the distillery a couple of times, and partnered with Chicago businessmen to expand the operation.

In advance of Prohibition, Jim decided to sell the distillery to three men, including Lambert Willett. Eventually, after many years, the warehouses here would be sold back to Beam, but Jim had already moved on. During Prohibition he dabbled in rock quarries, coal mining, and citrus groves, but upon repeal, he set up in Clermont, Kentucky, at the site of one of his rock quarries (and perhaps not entirely by coincidence, the defunct Murphy, Barber & Co. distillery). Jim helped rebuild the business after Prohibition and kept it alive with an unsentimental attitude. He partnered with city investors when necessary and bought, sold, and reorganized distilleries to build his brand. By the time of his death, the Beam family no longer owned Colonel James B. Beam Bourbon, but thanks to the advertising savvy of his investors in Chicago, it was one of the most popular brands in the United States, soon to become the undisputed leader in bourbon sales, a position it still holds.

He was a man of energy, according to the local paper, and had a sense of humor such that when the archbishop was supposed to visit, his wife organized a picnic in town. Beam and his friend and neighbor Leslie Samuels (see Bill and Margie Samuels, page 203) went to go pick him up and learned he'd had to cancel. Beam put on a hood and posed as the bishop to the great and public surprise of his wife.

After Jim's death, his son Jeremiah took over, and the brand and the distillery bounced around with new corporate owners from time to time; business grew steadily.

In 1965, Booker Noe, a grandson of Jim Beam, and Jeremiah's nephew, earned the leadership of the company as master distiller. But Booker wouldn't be a master distiller like any that had come before him. He would shift the position from one of factory management to whiskey innovator and, eventually, to public spokesman for his whiskeys.

To read Booker's son Fred's account of his growing up, Booker was intimately involved with running the factories, first at Boston and then later with the main distillery at Clermont. Booker had the idea that, as single-malt Scotch gained popularity, bourbon could also have a flavorful, more complex, and refined counterpart. Booker popularized his small-batch collection, consisting of brands built from small, select barrels.

It's fair to say that, these days, the title of master distiller is mostly a marketing position, and indeed wasn't really commonly used until after people started conflating the bourbon business with Scotch distillers. Master distillers are routinely seen signing bottles in the gift shop and traveling around the country (and sometimes around the world) doing promotional events for the brand. For most, if not all, of the commercial distilleries in Kentucky and Tennessee, decisions about the product are made by teams of engineers, chemists, marketing executives, and outside branding consultants. To be sure, no one with the last name of Beam or

Noe came up with the idea for Red Stag cherry-flavored bourbon. But Noe was creatively involved with those early innovations and helped build the idea of the distiller as a creative force in the business.

Noe belonged to an unusual moment in whiskey history when the chief distiller and chief marketer were the same person. If E. H. Taylor was one of the first of these men, then Pappy Van Winkle, Bill Samuels, and Noe were some of the last. Jimmy Russell, of Wild Turkey, is probably the last surviving distiller-marketer in the old model. These days, craft distillers are taking up the mantle, but it's admittedly an easier thing to innovate at one barrel a day, rather than one thousand.

In addition to distilling, Noe was obsessed with ham. He would hickory smoke and age hams behind his house, and would carry them on his trips for work in the trunk of his car. Fred Noe, in his book *Beam, Straight Up*, tells the story that when Booker was served a middling plate of ham at a respectable Chicago restaurant, he went out to the car and brought one of his own hams in, insisting that the chef try it, whereupon he ended up sharing it with half the restaurant. The story illustrates Booker as obsessive, meticulous, and charismatic, which best articulates the difference between a mere distiller and a masterful one.

David and Baker Beam pose for an ad in *Playboy* magazine in 1969

The bottling line at the James B. Beam distillery in 1949

FREDERICK STITZEL	WILLIAM LARUE WELLER	JULIAN "PAPPY" VAN WINKLE
DISTILLER AND INVENTOR	RECTIFIER AND WHISKEY BROKER	SALESMAN AND DISTILLER
1843–1924	1825–1899	1874–1965
———	———	———
Cave Hill Cemetery, Louisville, Kentucky	*Cave Hill Cemetery, Louisville, Kentucky*	*Cave Hill Cemetery, Louisville, Kentucky*

J ulian Van Winkle got his start at the William Larue Weller office. Weller was a rectifier, which means he mostly engaged in blending, cutting, bottling, and sometimes redistilling to improve whiskey other people had made. The Wellers had their own rectification column until 1873, when fire destroyed the distillery, after which they rented other distilleries in town to do the work. The Wellers mostly served as an intermediary between the distilleries, which created a bulk commodity, and to bars and saloons, which dispensed to customers. Rectifying allowed a distiller to make whiskey more homogenous and neutral. This is sometimes viewed today with disdain, but over history, tastes change: After full-flavored whiskeys (like single-malt Scotch and straight American whiskey) are in fashion for a while, there inevitably follows a shift in preference to lighter whiskeys (blended Scotch whiskey, Canadian whiskey, rectified whiskey). In the early 1870s, there was a fair amount of trickery going on with rectifiers adding flavors and colors, but it's possible that in the early days, this is something that people wanted.

Weller's family had been, like many Kentucky distillers, Maryland Catholics who started distilling near Bardstown, Kentucky, in the late 1700s. Daniel Weller, William's grandfather, died in 1807 with an inventory describing a very common frontier distillery. William Larue would arrive in Louisville and set up as a whiskey trader in 1849.

Weller had a reputation as an excellent whiskey broker; he placed his thumbprint on invoices so that customers would know they were getting the real thing (or perhaps this was just an excellent marketing move). He endured several setbacks, however: His brother Charles was killed by two gunmen while collecting on bills in Tennessee. Fire consumed his warehouse (and did so again in 1909, after his death). When Weller died in 1899, the business passed to his sons.

On or around 1893, a nineteen-year-old Julius P. Van Winkle joined W. L. Weller as a whiskey salesman. Pappy had attended Centre College, in Danville, but after his studies, he got into whiskey, probably to the disappointment of his father, a lawyer who briefly served as secretary of state.

Across town, in 1872, Philip and Frederick Stitzel, German brothers who arrived in Louisville in 1859, were building a series of distilleries, the first of which made only fifteen barrels a day. Frederick was something of an inventor, and he patented a warehousing system, three barrels high on each floor, that became widely used throughout Kentucky (and is still used today). Philip's son Arthur would inherit the business, and it was Arthur Philip Stitzel who would rent his distillery to the Weller labels.

So the Wellers had a reputation for selling whiskey, and the Stitzels had a reputation for making whiskey. Arthur formally entered into partnership with Julian Van Winkle and Alex Farnsley (another former Weller salesman) upon the repeal of Prohibition to create the Stitzel-Weller distillery, which was rebuilt from scratch in Shively, a suburb of Louisville (and outside the city's tax purview).

They had a boost from geography. During Prohibition, the Stitzel warehouses were turned into "consolidation warehouses" by the federal government, and barrels were shipped from the country, where they were hard to watch over, to urban areas in Louisville and Cincinnati, where presumably they were easier to keep under government supervision. This was a boon to Stitzel's prospects, as well as similar distilleries like Fleichmann's in Cincinnati. Stitzel had a license to manufacture and bottle medicinal spirits, and they may have been the first distillery to fire up the stills in 1929, as some distilleries were allowed to restart early, in order to replenish the supply of medicinal whiskey that had been

Warehouses at Stitzel-Weller

gradually drawing down from these urban consolidation warehouses (legitimately, and sometimes not).

The one thing they were missing was a brand. The Stitzel warehouses were full of barrels from other distilleries, many of them intended for bottling as major brands of the day: Cascade whiskey, Mammoth Cave, J. W. Dant, and Old Fitzgerald among them. S. C. Herbst in Milwaukee had inventory of Old Fitzgerald, and contracted with Stitzel to bottle it as medicinal whiskey as a way of getting rid of it. Van Winkle, who sensed that Prohibition wasn't going to last, wanted the Old Fitzgerald brand that Herbst wanted to get rid of. He bought the brand for ten thousand dollars.

Over the next thirty years, Van Winkle would grow the Old Fitzgerald, Rebel Yell, Mammoth Cave, and Cabin Still brands for sale throughout the country. When Farnsworth and Stitzel died, business was run by Van Winkle, his son Julian, and his son-in-law, King McClure. The master distiller was William H. McGill, whose sister was married to Joseph L. Beam. Stitzel-Weller was one of the smaller, independent distilleries at a time when most were owned by National, Seagram, or Schenley.

Van Winkle had a sign at Stitzel-Weller that is well known: "We make fine bourbon, at a profit if we can, at a loss if we must, but always fine bourbon." He had another sign that is less well known: "No Chemists Allowed! Nature and the old-time 'know how' of a Master Distiller get the job done here... This is a Distillery, not a whiskey factory." The anti-science attitude reflected an era when many distilleries were using enzymes and additives to improve production. Certain things do stand out about the Stitzel-Weller process: open fermentation, roller-milled corn, distillation to a low proof, and wheat as a flavor grain. Still, it's not clear that there was a huge difference between the way things were done at Stitzel and other distilleries.

Pappy's marketing—folksy, first-person essays about life in the country, which ran as advertisements in magazines like *Time* and the *New Yorker* in the 1950s and 1960s—are remarkable. Filled with a little subterfuge (Louisville was hardly the country), and some defensiveness (against "powder puff" blended whiskeys that were gaining favor in the era), his columns were squarely aimed at *men* in *business*.

The real heartbreak of Van Winkle's story comes at the end. He died in 1965, by all accounts oblivious to what was to come. With Van Winkle gone, the Farnsley side of the business, as well as McClure, wanted out. They suspected that distilling was to become the business of huge, international conglomerates, and the Van Winkles didn't feel like their distillery had a chance of surviving a wave of interest in lighter whiskeys and clear spirits. Pappy's son Julian was probably the best advocate for the company, but he was not strong enough to keep the company from being sold. (Indeed, all the family distilleries, save one—Heaven Hill—petered out in the 1970s; even Maker's Mark, the indie upstart, sold in 1982.) Today, most of the bourbon made in the United States is carried out by international companies, most of which are headquartered overseas. Stitzel-Weller was bought by Norton Simon, which was bought by Distillers Company Limited, which merged with Guinness to form United Distillers, which ultimately became Diageo, who operates the distillery today as a visitor center for its Bulleit brand, though it stopped production in 1992.

If there's a moral to the story, it is never trust your business to your kids. (This is not the only instance in this book where the moral applies.) But perhaps that is too harsh: In death, Van Winkle would have the last laugh. His son was smart enough to retain the warehouse receipts for a few barrels and held on to the Rip Van Winkle brand. He was not as good as Pappy at selling whiskey, doing most of his business selling bourbon in collectible decanters. And, in the 1980s, when bourbon was a tough sell, there was no reason to cash in those receipts, so the stock of bourbon gradually aged—and then one day, in 1996, the bourbon took top honors at the World Spirits Competition in Chicago.

At least that's the prevailing story; whether the whiskey that won the award has anything to do with what goes into bottles of Van Winkle Family Reserve today is a question worth asking (Van Winkle's grandson has said that the whiskey was a high-rye recipe from the long-defunct Old Boone Distillery). And the current Van Winkle marketing talks up

Julian Van Winkle in front of his office, 1961

the Van Winkle distillery, which is listed on the bottles even though it doesn't exist and, in a way, never did. Still, that doesn't seem to stop people from paying more than two thousand dollars for a bottle on the black market, which is the only way to get one.

More impressive than the whiskey that's sold today is Pappy himself, who straddled two important eras of whiskey history and he goes down in the annals of dead distillers, at least from Kentucky, with an important caveat, best articulated by Harry Harrison Kroll in 1967:

> To be a blue-blooded bourbon baron, you must be born one. You must have ancestors. Down at the Jim Beam factory Jeremiah Beam has them. Out at Owensboro the Medleys are loaded. At Star Hill Bill Samuels counts them on his fingers. The Browns at Brown-Forman, the Willetts, Creel Brown, the McKennas, when they sold H. McKenna, say their prayers to 'em. Even the Thompsons at Glenmore have two. You just can't beat the game. To be whiskey royalty, you must have generations of bourbon blood.
>
> But pause in your hasty conclusions. The mightiest distiller of all didn't have an ancestor to his name. That's the venerable Julian Van Winkle, otherwise "Pappy" Van Winkle, up at Old Fitzgerald in Louisville. He's a self-made bourbon baron, and a mighty warrior he's been these ninety years. Seventy-one of them he has been bourbonizing. It took a little time. But he exploded the myth of ancestry.

MARGIE
MATTINGLY
SAMUELS

TAYLOR
WILLIAM
SAMUELS

WHISKEY BRANDER

DISTILLER

1912–1985

1910–1992

Bardstown City Cemetery,
Bardstown, Kentucky

Bardstown City Cemetery,
Bardstown, Kentucky

When Bill Samuels graduated from engineering school in the 1930s, he was entering the whiskey business at the perfect time. Prohibition had been repealed and the American whiskey industry was starting over. But it wasn't an easy start. Most distilleries hadn't made whiskey in more than fifteen years, since before World War I. Machinery no longer worked, warehouses were empty, copper had been scrapped, and fermentation vats were covered in mold. Roofs leaked and windows were broken. The distilleries had to rebuild from scratch. And because whiskey takes time to mature, it was a long struggle to get bourbon of any quality. Just when American whiskey was starting to hit its stride, World War II halted production again.

It is sometimes told (on the distillery tour, for instance) that Samuels quit the bourbon business in the 1940s in disgust over the terrible whiskey his father was making. The truth is probably more nuanced.

Bill's father, Leslie, had operated a distillery near Bardstown before Prohibition and was set on rebuilding the family business, but he needed investors and so partnered with Robert Block in Cincinnati. All was going fine until Leslie died in 1936. Bill continued to work for the distillery and T. W. Samuels brand whiskey did quite well—so well that there were often shortages. The World War II restrictions on distilling disrupted the business at a critical time, and Block was forced to sell to investors in New York City. Without an ally on the business side of the distillery, Samuels decided to leave the company.

Samuels tried to market a new brand called Old Samuels whiskey, but he got sued by the new owners (for a corollary, see the dispute at Oscar Pepper, page 61) and lost, both in a lower court and on appeal in 1948. So if he were to enter the whiskey business, he would need a drastically new approach.

Samuels must have taken some time to figure this out. Surely he felt cheated out of an inheritance in an industry where distilleries were commonly passed down family lines over generations. He drifted, and his young wife, Margie, encouraged him to get his act together. According to family legend, Margie told him to "get off his ass." So Bill crafted a narrative that his father's whiskey had been of the bottom-shelf variety, distilled for yield over flavor. He wanted to make a more considered whiskey, and his wife had ideas for how to communicate that attention in detail to customers.

Bill bought the Burks Spring distillery, in Loretto, Kentucky, and the couple set about fixing it up to be the home of Maker's Mark. He consulted with an elder statesman, Julian "Pappy" Van Winkle at Stitzel-Weller, about bourbon recipes. Van Winkle seems to have told Bill pretty much everything, and indeed Maker's Mark continues to use open fermentation, roller-milled corn, distillation to a low proof, and wheat as a flavor grain—all idiosyncrasies of the Stitzel-Weller plant. The wheated recipe made a softer, more delicate whiskey, and the family bet that a mellower whiskey might play to a more sophisticated audience. Over time it found a wider audience, too.

Another lesson the Samuelses took from Van Winkle was in marketing. Van Winkle and his advertising agency (Winneas and Brandon, from Saint Louis) had developed a style of folksy first-person narratives that were written under his byline. Maker's Mark's famous line—"It tastes expensive . . . and is"—comes straight from the Pappy playbook.

Still, there were other things that couldn't be copied. Like branding. Initially, Bill and Margie pursued the name Star Hill Distilling Company. (If they couldn't use Bill's name, they would use the name of a family farm.) But it wasn't quite enough. Margie collected pewter and liked that each of the pewter makers had a distinctive identifying mark, often hidden in detail or on the bottom of a vessel. It showed the hand of the craftsman, and separated fine pewter from store-bought knockoffs. She considered the corollary with bourbon. She also collected old cognac bottles, and admired the wax that sealed them. She wanted Bill's whiskey to evoke not bourbons of the day, which weren't viewed with particular deference or respect, but European cognac, which had earned a solid reputation for quality over centuries. She proposed a wax seal, and labored over the family's deep fryer to try to get the perfect consistency and color. And lest you think Margie was a dowdy housewife, puttering about her collections, Margie had a degree in chemistry from the University of Louisville, which she applied to getting the wax just right. She settled on a bold arresting red that has defined the brand ever since.

At least, that's the way the story is told. Sam Cecil, once the master distiller at Maker's Mark and the author of *Bourbon: The Evolution of Kentucky Whiskey*, tells the story slightly differently. The Maker's Mark name, the red wax, and packaging were presented to Bill Samuels in 1957 by George Shields of the Saint Louis–based advertising agency French and Shields in a meeting at the University Club in Saint Louis. But who are we to get in the way of a good story?

Margie and Bill Samuels

A TOUR OF BARDSTOWN, KENTUCKY

BARDSTOWN IS THE BOURBON CAPITAL of the United States. While there are only two active distilleries in town, most of Kentucky's commercial distilleries are within a short drive, and many warehouses from defunct distilleries still hold aging whiskey off of side roads all around town. Many of Kentucky's great distillers are buried in Bardstown City Cemetery, or St. Joseph's, which is adjacent.

1. BARTON DISTILLERY
A large distillery owned by Sazerac, the Barton distillery (formerly the Tom Moore distillery) is an off-the-beaten-path stop on the bourbon trail

2. OSCAR GETZ MUSEUM
Mr. Getz, once a distiller at the Barton Distillery, collected whiskey memorabilia and this small museum has an interesting collection of bottles, documents, and other bourbon artifacts

3. JOHN FITCH
Built an early working steamboat, but failed to find commercial application; first interred in the old Bardstown Cemetery, his remains were moved to Courthouse Square

4. HEAVEN HILL
The distillery burned in 1996, but warehouses and the main office remain; a visitors center has a giant tasting room inside a barrel

5. JOSEPH WASHINGTON DANT
Log distiller, innovator, transitioned from frontier distiller to commerical enterprise; buried in the St. Francis Graveyard Cemetery

6. THOMPSON WILLETT
Started the Willett distillery; his grandchildren have reimagined the distillery as a craft producer

7. BILL SAMUELS
Created Maker's Mark from scratch after bad luck took the family business away from him

8. MARGIE SAMUELS
According to lore, Margie was an instrumental figure in coming up with the branding for Maker's Mark

9. JOSEPH L. BEAM
Prolific distiller, once ostracized to Mexico during Prohibition, his seven sons were all involved in whiskey-making

10. JIM BEAM
A canny, pragmatic distiller whose career spanned Prohibition and two world wars

11. BOOKER NOE
Jim Beam's grandson Booker Noe helped reinvent top-shelf bourbon in the 1980s and 1990s

12. FEDERAL HILL
Known colloquially as My Old Kentucky Home, Senator John Rowan's house was reportedly the inspiration for Kentucky's state song of that name, written by Stephen Foster

13. WILLETT DISTILLERY
Distillery started here after Prohibition but closed in the 1970s; a younger generation has reopened the distillery, making bourbon and rye

14. PIONEER CEMETERY
The older cemetery in Bardstown was used until the 1850s

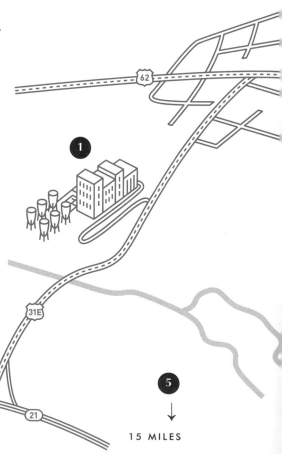

15 MILES

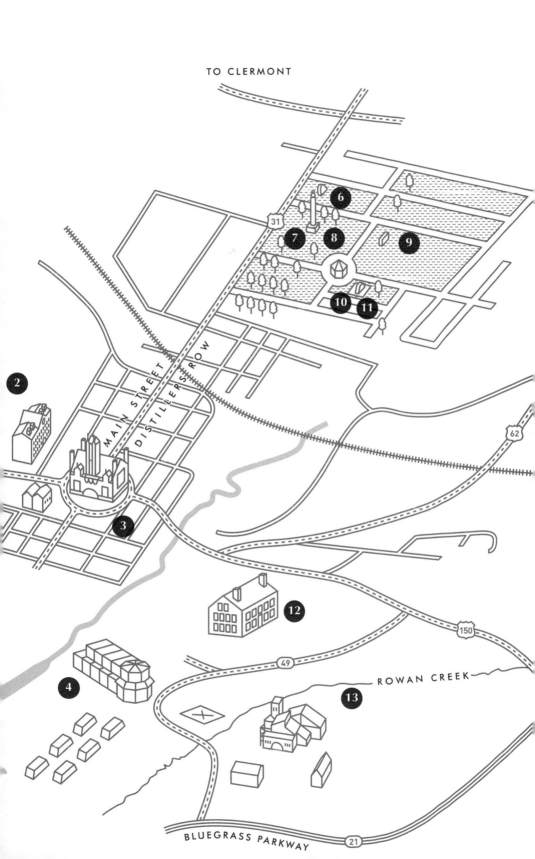

TO CLERMONT

31

6

7

8

9

10

11

MAIN STREET

DISTILLERS ROW

62

2

3

12

150

4

49

ROWAN CREEK

13

BLUEGRASS PARKWAY

21

LAWRENCE NEAVEAR	WILLIAM KOHLER	JAMES DANCEY
DISTILLER	DISTILLER	DISTILLER

MARION GARBER	RICHARD ERTMOED	EDWARD WINKLER
DISTILLER	DISTILLER	DISTILLER

ALL DIED 1954

Interred Lakeview Cemetery and Glendale Memorial Gardens, Pekin, Illinois

In 1954, a fire broke out at the American Distilling Company's plant in Pekin, Illinois, that raged for two days and consumed 110,000 barrels of aging whiskey. The fire broke out in one of the aging warehouses; it would eventually destroy three more. "The continuing fire, capped by a dazzling, nighttime, atomic-like explosion seen 75 miles away, destroyed much of the company's sprawling plant facilities in this central Illinois city," the Associated Press reported. "Damage is already well into the millions of dollars. The explosion last night lifted the roof and walls of one rackhouse—a six-story building—high into the air. The debris rained down on firemen and plant workers fighting to halt the fierce, whiskey-fed blaze touched off 17 hours earlier during a severe electrical storm." Six men died in the blaze, 33 others were injured. The distillery itself was spared (and was up and running less than a week after the incident).

Distillery fire at Heaven Hill in Bardstown, Kentucky, 1996

Mag Bailey's former home and bootlegging operation just outside Harlan, Kentucky

MAGGIE BAILEY

BOOTLEGGER

1904–2005

Resthaven Cemetery, near Harlan, Kentucky

Maggie Bailey, often called Mag or Mags, sold illegal liquor for nearly eighty years in Harlan County, Kentucky. Born on Line Fork Creek in Letcher County, she married briefly in her youth—even stole a police car on her honeymoon—but separated from her husband after eight years and settled down quickly to a quiet life of selling bootleg alcohol. She died at the age of 101 from complications of pneumonia.

Bailey herself was not a distiller. She sold moonshine, and in later years store-bought alcohol, from various outbuildings around her modest house about a half mile from town. She was also a broker of sorts: a financier and philanthropist, a liquor dealer selling in a dry county, a political figure. At one point, during Harlan County's coal boom in the 1930s, she was acting as a distributor to other bootleggers, selling moonshine in bulk to those who would sell it by the half pint. Recognizing her importance, a candidate for governor, Albert B. "Happy" Chandler, stopped in once and offered to buy her some new shoes if she would help him get elected. After he won, a package arrived with a new pair of shoes.

Bailey did spend some time in a women's correctional facility during World War II, which convinced her to abandon selling moonshine, favoring store-bought whiskeys (on which tax had already been paid), according to her lawyers. She also had a sister who worked for National Distillers in Louisville, who sent her hand-me-down uniforms. Deeply frugal herself, Bailey saved most of the money she ever earned, and used the proceeds to give to friends and customers in the neighborhood to buy warm clothes and coal for heat in the winter.

Her cash reserve did cause her some difficulty in the 1960s, when police found one hundred to two hundred thousand dollars (depending on whose accounting is to be trusted) in footlockers in her house. Bailey defended her cash hoard by saying she lost money in the banks in the panic of 1929 and hadn't used them since. Still, in later years, her trouble was not for bootlegging (a criminal activity for local courts), but for tax evasion (a federal matter).

Time and time again, Bailey would beat charges levied against her, and, eventually, police and prosecutors gave up. Her lawyer's strategy was always: *Could this woman ever hurt anyone?* Juries believed she could not. And so she was able to carry on, essentially filling the void created by county statutes.

She was wary. She would ask newcomers, "Whose boy are you?" or something to that effect (a tradition her nephew still employs if you happen to make a pilgrimage to her house). In later years, she hired help to run the operation, which resembled a drive-through liquor store.

A fictionalized version of Bailey was played by Margo Martindale on the television series *Justified*. Harlan voted to allow sales of alcohol for on-premise consumption in restaurants in the late 2000s, and now the Portal, a sort of coal mining–themed restaurant, has a tagline written on the wall: "If Mags could see us now."

LEWIS SOLON ROSENSTIEL

BOOTLEGGER,
DISTILLERY OWNER

1891–1976

---

*Walnut Hills Cemetery,
Cincinnati, Ohio*

SIDNEY FRANK

DISTILLED SPIRITS
SALESMAN

1919–2006

---

*Walnut Hills Cemetery,
Cincinnati, Ohio*

Lew Rosenstiel was kicked in the head during a high school football game when he was sixteen, and he was sent to recuperate from his eye injury in the countryside at his cousin's house in Milton, Kentucky. His uncle David ran a distillery there, just a few miles downriver on the Kentucky side of the river. To help Lew pass the time, he hired him in the cafeteria; Lew took to the distillery and his ambitions of becoming a doctor soon faded.

Rosenstiel was good at predicting the future. He guessed Prohibition wouldn't last and did everything he could to buy stocks of whiskey, distilleries, and contracts so that he could reenter the market when the time was right. His company, Schenley Industries, was built off that prediction. (He also predicted high-speed underwater travel, but probably a good thing he didn't invest as heavily in that.)

Rosenstiel beat bootlegging charges in 1929, and only later, as a result of a 1970s-era investigation into organized crime, would his connection to Meyer Lansky and other Prohibition figures come out.

In the late stages of Prohibition, Rosenstiel acquired several distilleries and brands, most notably a now-defunct distillery just north of where MGP is in Lawrenceburg today, an evolution of the old Squibb distillery. Known as Schenley, the distillery made Old Quaker rye, Golden Wedding rye, and others. Schenley also distilled at other distilleries and distributed George T. Stagg, James E. Pepper, John T. Barbee, Blanton Distilling Company, and others.

Rosenstiel was friendly with J. Edgar Hoover and a lawyer named Roy Cohn, who briefly owned the Lionel toy train company, served as an investigative lawyer to Senator Joe McCarthy, and would be remembered as a character in *Angels in America*, the Tony Kushner play about the AIDS crisis.

Rosenstiel was often the subject of rumors about wild sexual exploits in hotel rooms, often involving Hoover and Cohn, though the source, Rosenstiel's fourth wife, Susan, served time in prison for perjury and is generally discredited. (While it's probably true that all three men had sexual preferences that were not accepted in their time, Hoover's "cross-dressing" is widely regarded as a myth, traceable entirely to Susan.) Hoover's reluctance to address organized crime while he was in office, however, may have had to do with certain crime figures having evidence by which they could blackmail him, which may also explain why Rosenstiel's shady Prohibition-era past never interfered with his legitimate business. In any event, there was a web of secrecy, liquor money, and politics that gave Rosenstiel an avenue to success after Prohibition.

Rosenstiel gave much of his wealth to charity, including medical research. While he lay comatose and dying in a hotel room in Miami, Cohn tried to get him to sign a revised will that would have named him and Rosenstiel's granddaughter Cathy Frank as beneficiaries, but the scratches were later ruled an invalid signature by the New York State Supreme Court, resulting in Cohn's being disbarred only weeks before his death, in 1986.

Cathy Frank's husband, Sidney, had been involved with the business, but, after a dispute with Lew, he was forced from the company. Striking out on his own, he secured importation rights to a then obscure liqueur brand, Jägermeister, and built it into an empire. Following that, he created and sold the brand Grey Goose to Bacardi in 2004 for $2.3 billion.

KYLE ROGERS

HARDIN, KY *– Officials say a 27-year-old man who was injured in an explosion and a fire at a western Kentucky distillery last month has died at the Nashville hospital where had been since. The Paducah Sun reports Kyle Rogers died Monday. He had been in critical condition in the burn unit since an explosion at the Silver Trail Distillery in Hardin, April 25.*

On the distillery's Facebook page, Silver Trail founder Spencer Balentine said: "Kyle carved his name on our hearts and left a legacy etched in our minds and then like all moonshine legends before him…he was gone."

Page 3. Vintage postcard; **4-5.** Wild Turkey Distillery; **9.** Green-Wood Archives; **12.** (top and bottom) Library of Congress; **15.** (top and bottom) Monumental Bronze Company; **20-21.** Museum of the City of New York; **25.** Engraving by Theodore de Bry from a woodcut by Matthäus Merian; **27.** New York Public Library Digital Collection; **30.** Painting by Pompeo Batoni / Utah Museum of Fine Arts; **32-33.** *The Dream or the True History of Deacon Giles' Distillery and Deacon Jones' Brewery: Reported for the Benefit of Posterity,* George Barrell Cheever (New York: Printed for the publishers, 1848); **35.** Painting by Gilbert Stuart / National Portrait Gallery; **37.** National Archives; **38.** Mount Vernon; **49.** New York Historical Society; **51.** Daguerreotype by Matthew Brady / National Archives; **52.** Hermitage Distillery promotional advertisement; 58. Lincoln Memorial University; **62.** Kentucky Historical Society; **65.** Hillforest Historical Foundation; **70.** Kings County Distillery Boozeum; **73, 76, 82.** National Archives; **85.** Dant Family Collection; **86-87.** Filson Historical Society; **90, 93** (left and right). Brown-Forman Archives; **94.** Buffalo Trace Distillery; **95.** Chicago Tribune/PARS; **99, 100-101.** Corbis; **109.** Wikicommons; **114.** Kentucky Historical Society; **116.** Brown-Forman Archives; **117.** Buffalo Trace Archives; **119, 120.** Vintage postcard; **122-123.** Lafayette Studios Collection, Kentucky Digital Library; **125.** Photo by Carleton E Watkins; **129.** Museum of the City of New York; **130.** From *The Story of the Bernheim Family* by I. W. Bernheim (Louisville, KY: J.P. Morton & Co., 1910); **131.** From *Preyer's information and Guide for the Liquor Business* (New York: [s.n.], 1901); **132-133.** University of Louisville Archives; **136.** Lafayette Studios Collection, Kentucky Digital Library; **140.** From *Jokichi Takamine: A Record Of His American Achievements* (New York: William Edwin Rudge, 1928); **144.** DC Public Library; **149.** Chicago Tribune Archives; **150.** found photo; **152** (top and bottom). Joe W. Boone; **153.** Wild Turkey Distillery; **159.** Delhi Historical Society; **161.** Corbis; **169.** Chicago Tribune Archives; **173.** The Mariner's Museum, Newport News, VA; **176-177.** New York City Municipal Archives; **180.** Vintage postcard; **182.** Heaven Hill Archives; **184-185.** Kentucky Historical Society; **186, 187.** Georgia Racing Hall of Fame; **193.** Beam/Suntory Archives; **194-195.** University of Louisville Archives; **198, 201.** Lin Caufield photograph courtesy University of Louisville Photo Archives; **205.** Maker's Mark Archives; **210.** Kings County Distillery Archives

Heesang Lee: **pp. 22-23, 44-45, 68-69, 112-113, 164-165, 206-207, 222-223**

ACKNOWLEDGEMENTS

This book owes a great debt to Chelsea Dowell at Green-Wood Cemetery, who first suggested the idea of a tour of dead distillers followed by a tasting at our distillery. Likewise, Ruth Edebohls, who leads several tours at Green-Wood, has been helpful in researching distillers. In Kentucky, Mike Veach shared his knowledge during a great tour of distillers in Cave Hill Cemetery, along with Michael Higgs who helped provide resources for this book. Steve Beam, a descendant of many distillers, was very generous with his time. We also would like to thank other distiller's descendants—Greg Dant, Georgia Dant, Fred Noe, Rachel Lambert, and Drew Kulsveen—for offering their time and knowledge.

For images, we are thankful to Ian Hunter at Deacon Giles distillery, Pam Yeager at the University of Louisville, Stacy Locke at Green-Wood, and especially Rory Walsh, for researching and collecting hundreds of images that tell a much bigger story than could be included in this book.

We are grateful to David Kuhn, Nicole Tourtelot, and Kate Mack for making this book happen, and to Deb Aaronson for championing it. At Abrams, David Cashion, Deb Wood, and John Gall were masterful partners with exquisite taste.

Thanks also to the team at Kings County for their hard work and curiosity, prompting us always to be thinking critically about whiskey and its history, and to our colleagues at craft distilleries around the country for the renewed cultural interest in distilling that makes unearthing forgotten distillers all the more rewarding.

BIBLIOGRAPHY

On cemeteries:

Last Great Necessity, The: Cemeteries in American History, David Charles Sloane (John Hopkins University Press, 1991)

Lincoln at Gettysburg: The Words That Remade America, Garry Wills (Simon & Schuster, 1992)

Rest in Peace: A History of American Cemeteries, Meg Greene (Twenty-First Century Books, 2008)

Information on graves that we did not visit in person is taken from www.findagrave.com.

On distilling history:

Beverages and Their Adulteration, Harvey Washington Wiley, (P. Blakiston, Son & Co., 1919)

Bluegrass, Belles, and Bourbon: A Pictorial History of Whiskey in Kentucky, Harry Harrison Kroll (A. S. Barnes and Co., 1967)

Bourbon: A History of the American Spirit, Dane Huckelbridge (William Morrow, 2014)

Bourbon: The Evolution of Kentucky Whiskey, Sam K. Cecil (Turner Publishing, 2010)

Bourbon, Strange: Surprising Stories of American Whiskey, Charles K. Cowdery (Made and Bottled in Kentucky, 2014)

Bourbon Empire: The Past and Future of America's Whiskey, Reid Mitenbuler (Viking, 2015)

Kentucky Bourbon: The Early Years of Whiskeymaking, Henry G. Crowgey (University Press of Kentucky, 2008)

Kentucky Bourbon Whiskey: An American Heritage, Michael R. Veach (University Press of Kentucky, 2013)

Moonshine: A Cultural History of America's Infamous Liquor, Jaime Joyce (Zenith Press, 2014)

Preyer's Information and Guide for the Liquor Business, Edgar Reuben Preyer (Edgar R. Preyer, 1901)

Whiskey Rebellion, The: George Washington, Alexander Hamilton, and the Frontier Rebels Who Challenged America's Newfound Sovereignty, William Hogeland (Simon & Schuster, 2006)

On specific distillers:

Bahama Queen, The: Prohibition's Daring Beauty, Gertrude C. Lythgoe (Flat Hammock Press, 2007 reprint of 1964 text)

Beam, Straight Up: The Bold Story of the First Family of Bourbon, Fred Noe with Jim Kokoris (John Wiley & Sons, 2012)

Blood & Whiskey: The Life and Times of Jack Daniel, Peter Krass (John Wiley & Sons, 2004)

Blood & Wine: The Unauthorized Story of the Gallo Empire, Ellen Hawkes (Simon & Schuster, 1993)

Bronfmans, The: The Rise and Fall of the House of Seagram, Nicholas Faith (Thomas Dunne, 2006)

But Always Fine Bourbon: Pappy Van Winkle and the Story of Old Fitzgerald, Sally Van Winkle Campbell (Old Rip Van Winkle Distillery, 2014)

Dark Tide: The Great Boston Molasses Flood of 1919, Stephen Puleo (Beacon Press, 2004)

Declaration of the State of the Colonie and Affaires in Virginia, A, Edward Waterhouse, accessed from encyclopediavirginia.org (Original text 1622)

Gallo Be Thy Name: The Inside Story of How One Family Rose to Dominate the U.S. Wine Market, Jerome Tuccille (Phoenix Books, 2009)

Good Spirits: The Making of a Businessman, Edgar M. Bronfman (G. P. Putnam's Sons, 1998)

History of Kentucky, Lewis Collins (Collins & Co., 1882)

Jokichi Takamine (1854–1922) and Caroline Hitch Takamine (1866–1954): Biography and Bibliography, William Shurtleff and Akiko Aoyagi, ed. (Soyinfo Center, 2012)

King of the Bootleggers: A Biography of George Remus, William A. Cook (McFarland & Co., 2008)

Lives of Virginia Baptist Ministers, James B. Taylor (Sheldon & Company, 1860)

Overholt (A.) & Co.: A History of the Company and the Overholt Family, 1940, Karen Rose Overholt Critchfield, ed., accessed via Overholt Genealogy Website (www.karensbranches.com)

Papers of Andrew Jackson, Volume 1, 1770-1803, The, Sam B. Smith & Harriet Chappell Owsley, ed. (University of Tennessee Press, 1980)

Seasons of Misery: Catastrophe and Colonial Settlement in Early America, Kathleen Donegan (University of Pennsylvania Press, 2013)

Story of the Bernheim Family, The, Isaac Wolfe Bernheim, (John P. Morton & Company, 1910)

Thomas Mellon and His Times, Thomas Mellon (University of Pittsburgh Press, 1994)

Social History:

Cane Ridge: America's Pentecost, Paul K. Conkin (University of Wisconsin Press, 1990)

Secrets of the Internal Revenue, The, U. S. Vidocq [pseudonum], Franklin Eliot Felton, ed. (William Flint, 1869)

Dry Manhattan: Prohibition in New York City, Michael A. Lerner (Harvard University Press, 2007)

How the Other Half Lives, Jacob A. Riis (Dover Publications, 1971)

Island at the Center of the World, The: The Epic Story of Dutch Manhattan and the Forgotten Colony That Shaped America, Russell Shorto (Vintage Books, 2005)

Last Call: The Rise and Fall of Prohibition, Daniel Okrent (Scribner, 2010)

Mint Juleps with Teddy Roosevelt: The Complete History of Presidential Drinking, Mark Will-Weber (Regency Publishing, 2014)

Pure Food: Securing the Federal Food and Drugs Act of 1906, James Harvey Young (Princeton University Press, 1989)

Whiskey Women: The Untold Story of How Women Saved Bourbon, Scotch, and Irish Whiskey, Fred Minnick (Potomac Books, 2013)

Pictorial Histories:
Bardstown, Dixie Hibbs (Arcadia Publishing, 1998)
Book of Bourbon and Other Fine American Whiskeys, The, Gary Regan and Mardee Haidin Regan (Chapters Publishing Ltd., 1995)
Cave Hill Cemetery: A Pictorial Guide and History of Louisville's "City of the Dead," Samuel W. Thomas (Cave Hill Cemetery, 1985)
Green-Wood Cemetery, Alexandra Kathryn Mosca (Arcadia Publishing, 2008)
Kentucky Bourbon Trail, The, Berkeley and Jeanine Scott (Arcadia Publishing, 2009)
Whiskey: An American Pictorial History, Oscar Getz (David McKay Company, 1978)

Periodicals:
Atlanta Constitution, "Distiller Converted and Joins Church," April 28, 1909 (Jack Daniel)
Brooklyn Daily Eagle, "Nancy the Moonshiner—A Story of New Jersey and Its Applejack," February 2, 1896
Corbin Times-Tribune, "Harlan's Leading Bootlegger Has Plenty of Friends," May 31, 1972 (Mag Bailey)
Courier-Journal (Louisville, KY), "At Atlanta—The Remains of Paul Jones May Rest," February 25, 1895 (Paul Jones); "Remains of W. L. Wller Sent from Ocala Fla., Yesterday," March 25, 1899 (W. L. Weller)
Delphos Daily Herald, "Leaps to Death in California," April 2, 1945 (I. W. Bernheim)
Fresno Bee, "Fresno Farmer and Wife Victims of Murder and Suicide," June 21, 1933 (Joseph Gallo)
Esquire, "The Poison Squad: An Incredible History," Bruce Watson, June 27, 2013 (Harvey Washington Wiley); "The Last American Hero Is Junior Johnson. Yes!" Tom Wolfe, March 1965 (Lloyd Seay)
Galveston Daily News, "Moonshine Mary Is Convicted in Death," March 22, 1924 (Mary Wazeniak)
Index-Journal (Greenwood, SC), "Stock Car Racing Now Is Big Business," Paul Hemphill, November 17, 1970 (Lloyd Seay)
Internal Revenue Record and Customs Journal, July 22, 1871 (Clinton Gilbert)
Long Island Historical Journal, "Moonshiners in Brooklyn: Federal Authority Confronts Urban Culture, 1869–1880," Wilbur Miller, Vol 2, No. 2.
Los Angeles Herald, "Distilling Brandy, the Grape Growers' Distillery Hard at Work," October 8, 1886 (L. J. Rose)
New York Times, "James Crow, Whisky Maker," September 9, 1897; "The Whiskey War: A Military Expedition to 'Irishtown'*Oakland Tribune*, "Woman Fights Woman—Lady Bootleggers and Feminine Sleuths Tilt as the Fair Sex Goes to the Front Line with the Sock Troops of the Rum War," August 5, 1928 (Gertrude Lythgoe)
Philadelphia Times, "The Whiskey Inquiry," February 9, 1893 (Joseph Greenhut)

Rutland County Herald, "The Cause of Temperance," July 6, 1840 (W. H. Harrison)

San Francisco Chronicle, "Suicide of L. J. Rose—Noted Los Angeles Man Ends His Life with Morphine," May 18, 1899 (L. J. Rose)

Santa Ana Register, "Former Rum Row Queen Haunted by Fear of Jinx," June 10, 1926 (Gertrude Lythgoe)

Slate, "The Chemist's War," Deborah Blum, February 19, 2010 (Mary Wazeniak)

Sports Illustrated, "The Legend Lloyd Seay Was the Young Sport's Brightest Star Until He Was Gunned Down," Ed Hinton, January 28, 1998 (Lloyd Seay)

Tipton Daily Tribune, "Assignment America," Phillis Battelle, May 22, 1958 (Lewis Rosenstiel)

Film:

Prohibition, Ken Burns and Lynn Novick, 2011

Websites:

hillforest.org (Thomas Gaff)

montanawomenshistory.org (Birdie Brown)

pre-prowhiskeymen.blogspot.com (Louis Fleischmann, Thomas Gaff, Mary Dowling)

sippincorn.blogspot.com (James Crow, E. H. Taylor)

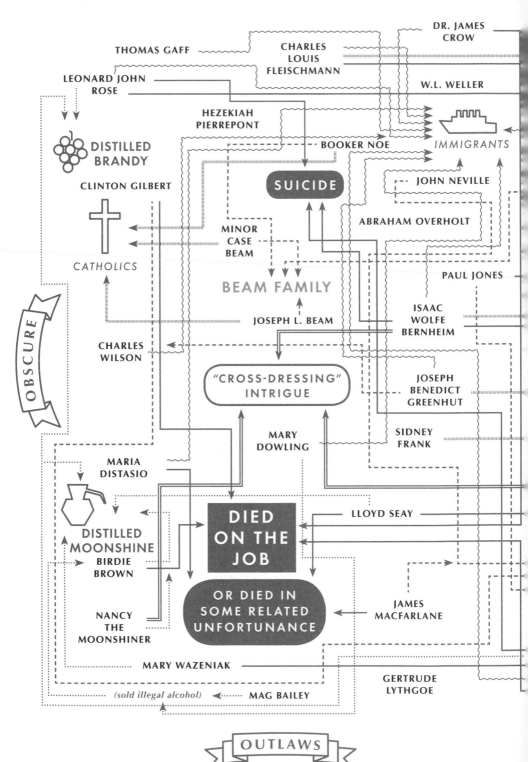

DR. JAMES CROW

THOMAS GAFF

CHARLES LOUIS FLEISCHMANN

LEONARD JOHN ROSE

W.L. WELLER

HEZEKIAH PIERREPONT

IMMIGRANTS

BOOKER NOE

DISTILLED BRANDY

CLINTON GILBERT

SUICIDE

JOHN NEVILLE

ABRAHAM OVERHOLT

MINOR CASE BEAM

CATHOLICS

PAUL JONES

BEAM FAMILY

JOSEPH L. BEAM

ISAAC WOLFE BERNHEIM

CHARLES WILSON

"CROSS-DRESSING" INTRIGUE

JOSEPH BENEDICT GREENHUT

MARY DOWLING

SIDNEY FRANK

MARIA DISTASIO

DISTILLED MOONSHINE

BIRDIE BROWN

DIED ON THE JOB

LLOYD SEAY

OR DIED IN SOME RELATED UNFORTUNANCE

JAMES MACFARLANE

NANCY THE MOONSHINER

MARY WAZENIAK

GERTRUDE LYTHGOE

(sold illegal alcohol) ◄ MAG BAILEY

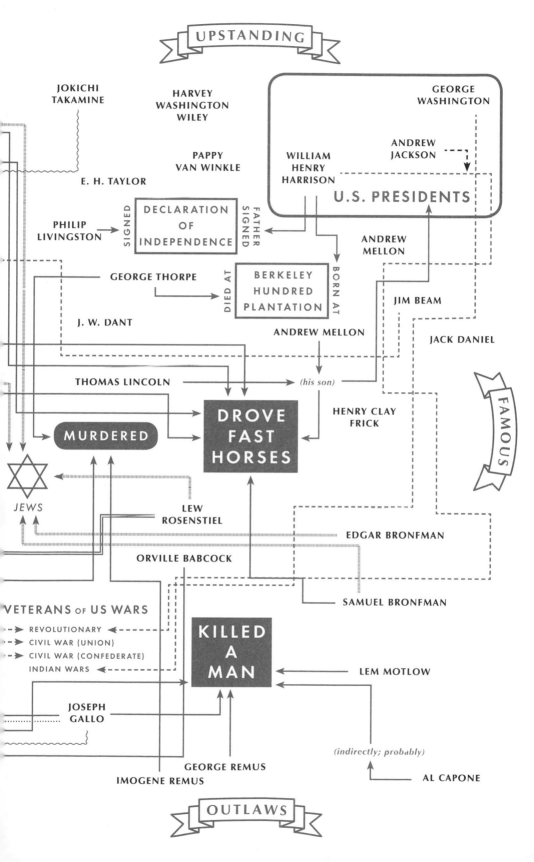

Editor: David Cashion
Designer: Deb Wood
Production Manager: Anet Sirna-Bruder

Library of Congress Control Number:
2015949272

ISBN: 978-1-4197-2021-5

Printed and bound in the United States
10 9 8 7 6 5 4 3 2 1

Abrams Image books are available at
special discounts when purchased in
quantity for premiums and promotions
as well as fundraising or educational
use. Special editions can also be created
to specification. For details, contact
specialsales@abramsbooks.com or the
address below.

ABRAMS
THE ART OF BOOKS SINCE 1949
115 West 18th Street
New York, NY 10011
www.abramsbooks.com